Plan Be!

Plan Be!

Awesome Inspiration for Your Awesome Life

BECCA ANDERSON

Author of bestselling *The Book of Awesome Women*

Mango Publishing
CORAL GABLES

For permission requests, please contact the publisher at:
Mango Publishing Group
2850 Douglas Road, 3rd Floor
Coral Gables, FL 33134 U.S.A
info@mango.bz

For special orders, quantity sales, course adoptions and corporate sales,
please email the publisher at sales@mango.bz. For trade and wholesale
sales, please contact Ingram Publisher Services at
customer.service@ingramcontent.com or +1.800.509.4887.

Plan Be!: Awesome Inspiration for Your Awesome Life

Library of Congress Cataloging
ISBN: (paperback) 978-1-63353-754-5, (ebook) 978-1-63353-755-2
Library of Congress Control Number: 2018941611
BISAC category code: SEL004000 SELF-HELP / Affirmations

Printed in the United States of America

This book is dedicated to all the amazing women from whom I have learned so much, and many of them are quoted here. Women helping other women will save the world!

For love casts out fear, and gratitude can conquer pride.

—Louisa May Alcott

Contents

Foreword

Wisdom, Thy Name Is Woman

The volume you hold in your hands is a wonderful compilation of quips and quotes by inspiring women. They are mothers, sisters, daughters, aunts, grandmas, girlfriends, neighbors, classmates, and coworkers.

Some are famous—others not. But they all have uttered words that can teach, console, lift us up out of our doldrums, and share wisdom for our journey through life, and this is a book to turn to again and again for advice, support, encouragement, empathy, and understanding.

As you'll see, wisdom isn't limited to those of fame and fortune. Some of the wisest words I've ever heard came from the lips of ordinary women of extraordinary insight, like Suzanne Schultz, a researcher at the University of Delaware, who once said, "The greatest gift you can give someone is the gift of the interested listener." Or my dear friend Karen, who likes to say, "Don't let what you can't do stop you from what you can do." My female friends and colleagues may come and go, but their wise words stay with me forever.

That's not to say that famous women aren't great sources of inspiration, too, because they are. For sure. And this book offers you the gift of their words as well.

Becca Anderson's collection, *Plan Be*, is a veritable treasure chest of pearls of wisdom and wit from women. Words to live by—words to love by—words to laugh by. Words of wisdom from women who fan the flame of hope that each of us can design the kind of life we want to live—we don't have to buy into anyone else's definition of success, happiness, or fulfillment.

These are pearls of great worth. Try them on—see how they feel—choose the pearls that best suit you and the kind of life you aspire to. Keep them close to your heart. Every woman needs a good string of pearls...pearls of wisdom, that is.

Barbara Jean Hateley

Introduction

Plan Be!
Secrets of Highly Successful Women

Women inspire me. It's as simple as that. All I have to do is look around. There are the women who run the restaurant on the corner—the place where everybody feels comfortable and taken care of. There are mothers pushing strollers, and mothers crunching numbers. There are women healing the sick. Gals cracking us up. Ladies penning the novels and singing the songs that change our lives. Chicks fixing the plumbing. Girls setting world records. Politicians challenging the status quo from within the system, and activists battering it from the outside. There are women at the pinnacle of their fields in every corner of the world, and women finding satisfaction in their own successes, small and large. What's their secret? (Well, I'll give you a hint…there's more than one.)

What kind of success are you working toward?

Maybe you don't know yet—or thought you did but aren't sure. Or maybe you're on the right track but need a kick in the pants.

In our own lives, success can feel elusive. We can get
bogged down comparing ourselves to others or whining
about what we lack. The women in this book have secrets
to share, to shout to the rafters even. Their wise words
will push your buttons, open your eyes, and rev up
your engine.

This book is a reminder that you have what it takes
to make it to the top. And the best part is, you get to
decide where the top is, and you get to chart the path
to reach it. This book is here for you—it's full of quotes
and thoughts from hundreds of women to encourage,
motivate, and support you as you make your way. Famous
and infamous, wise and wisecracking, haughty and humble.
Some are names you will know well, others are everyday
gals like you and me with something important to add.

☺
—
12

I read somewhere that we're all descended from three
ancestral mothers. How amazing is that? A woman
brought each and every one of us into this world, and
when we look in the mirror, we can see traces of our
mothers, grandmothers, even great-grandmothers. And
their gifts go way beyond skin-deep. Every woman in
the world is a member of this family—and you can call
on their words and their life stories to inspire you at
every turn. So keep this book close to you as you get
organized, vamp up your personal style, and figure out
how to work smarter. Sit back and let this book help
you remember the importance of relaxing and indulging

yourself (with girlfriends whenever possible). And don't ever forget to go after your dreams with every ounce of yourself, because after all—women can do anything!

The Art of Self-Affirmation

If you find yourself feeling overwhelmed and drained by the busyness of life with its many demands, you need to stop in your tracks and do an attitude adjustment, or more specifically, a "gratitude adjustment." Whenever you have gotten to this point, you have need of some "me TLC" and a dose of radical self-care. Chances are, your very wonderfulness may have led you to give and give and give and give. Now, you need to give and give and give to yourself. You need to soak up the glory of your very being and remember that you are an amazing, awesome person and deserving of all good things!

☺
—
13

The world is changing all around us with increasing speed, making most of us feel we have no control. We are so busy doing and being productive and bullet journaling our way through life that we might be riding on the back of our own bus. Positive living and affirmation queen Becca Anderson has been to the edge of overwhelm and back again. While on her journey, she has gathered a lot of wisdom, and here is her big takeaway:

If you affirm yourself every day, you can rule the world. More importantly, you can live a life filled with love, joy, fulfillment, and satisfaction thanks to your own positive self-regard.

Through the art of daily self-affirmation, you can take control of your own destiny and create your ideal life. If it sounds easy, it can be, but it does require you to develop the discipline to reflect on a positive affirmation each day. These affirmations are a mindfulness practice that will strengthen your self-esteem. Like a muscle, the more you do it, the stronger your confidence and sense of self will be. *Plan Be!* is the ultimate motivating, encouraging, and uplifting book to enjoy and share. These very wise words and affirmative sayings have the power to touch our hearts, make us laugh, and alleviate our stress as we realize the vast potential life has to offer. Grouped together, these quips, quotes, and "power thoughts" can help you deal with everything life throws at you with élan. Simply put, you'll be too blessed to be stressed!

How to Use This Book

Pick up the book, randomly open to a quote, and let those words be your guiding thought for the day. If you are REALLY resonating to this power thought, keep using it every day and let it become your mantra.

Use these inspired ideas in speeches, on your bulletin board, in your email signature, your Twitter handle, and on your social media. Hey, if it is your favorite ever Big Thought, get a tattoo on your inner wrist where you see it all the time and are reminded of your personal worth and of the great big beautiful world we all live in.

Read a few and really "power up" for your day, sort of like a booster shot in word form. If you are getting ready to do a presentation, a sales pitch, or an interview for your dream job, your next YouTube taping, or any very important date, these affirmations can be the wind in your sails.

Just love the heck out of yourself EVERY day!

☺

Chapter One

Organization Is the Key to Happiness

Do you come home every night and feel a bit guilty about the stacks and piles of clutter? Is something blocking your creativity or the get-up-and-go you need for all your household projects? Does your energy feel "stuck" in certain rooms, even impeding a good night's sleep in your own bed? Do you go out or order in dinner all the time, not even wanting to cook in your own kitchen? If any of this rings true, I wrote this book for you. Is your desk or workstation hopelessly cluttered?

Your home and office should feel like a sanctuary. We should be able to walk in the front door and immediately feel a sense of comfort, refuge, and safe haven. There are lots of things you can do, both large and small, that will make a tangible difference in the way your home feels and functions. Getting rid of anything you no longer use will increase the functionality of your home by making it easier to clean, increase orderliness, and also improve energies. I made a breakthrough discovery two years ago when I decided to unpack boxes I had never opened since moving in six years before. While they were tucked away unseen in the basement storage area, I knew they were there. One weekend, I decided to take the plunge and open those boxes. Going through our things can be an emotional experience; I remember finding a card from a friend who had passed away and immediately becoming misty-eyed. Powered by a triple latte, I plowed through the boxes and placed objects into three designated areas: Donate, Trash, and Keep. The goal was to have as little in the "keep" zone as possible. I am proud to say that even less was in the trash, and that was only a few items that broke during the move. "Donate" became several carloads to the Recycle and Reuse Center. Once I got the knack of it, most of the "Keep" pile ended up there, too. After the whirl of activity, something unexpected happened: I felt suddenly very buoyant and much lighter. I realized those unopened boxes had caused an invisible cloud of guilt; they had weighed me down. When the cloud lifted, I experienced a kind of effervescent joy. It was simply wonderful. I ask you, what might be holding you back from being utterly happy at home or at work?

If managing your life feels like a war, then half of every battle is getting things in order. For me, it's no fun at all. I have this nagging feeling that I have two lives going on simultaneously: the fun stuff and the rest of it. For example, I love to cook but despise washing dishes. I love the feeling of paying off the monthly bills, but often can't get myself together to do it until a week past the deadline, and then I feel miserable about the cumulative effect on my credit score. And any upheaval—a move, an emergency, or just getting a bad head cold—throws me for a loop. *How did I let this go?!* I ask myself, crazed. *Why is my house filled with paper?!* (One in every five pieces is really important, I swear.)

Well, it's time for a detox, a deep cleansing, and a spring cleaning. Doing your taxes. Clearing and sorting your wardrobe. Getting rid of the magazines you've been unwittingly storing since college. What a wonderful release. Now, those are the big projects, and don't worry yourself into trying to do them all at once. Just pick a project each month and do it a little at a time, or else set aside a whole weekend to blast through, whatever suits your style.

And for the rest of the month, take aim at the little, repetitive, everyday stuff. Work hard to make it a habit to sort your mail right away, clean out your pockets and purse every day, and dream up new ways to multitask effectively. Train yourself to make a difference in tiny ways all day long, and soon you'll forget it's an annoyance, because when it all adds up, you're way ahead of the game. If you can coax yourself into making the art of organization second nature, I promise it will serve you forever.

☺
—
19

FIND YOUR FOCUS

You may not be able to foresee
what the universe has planned for you, but
that doesn't mean your own plans should
be unpredictable.

—SANDRA OLIVER

Sometimes I still lose my head, even though
it is attached to my body. But if I've left
myself a note, I can usually find it again.

—MARLO THOMAS

Detail is electric.

—BONNI GOLDBERG

To know where you can find a thing is the
chief part of learning.

—UNKNOWN

Only when your consciousness is totally
focused on the moment you are in can
you receive whatever gift, lesson, or
delight that moment has to offer.

—BARBARA DE ANGELIS

On clutter: chaos begets chaos in our
homes, and in our minds.

—CAROL WISEMAN

☺
—
21

A place for everything,
and everything in its place.

—ISABELLA MARY BEETON

Just before bedtime prayers, evaluate each
day. Make plans for tomorrow that will
move you toward your long-range goal.

—FLORENCE S. JACOBSEN

Words are a lens to focus one's mind.

—AYN RAND

Most of what you obtain in life will be because of your discipline. Discipline is perhaps more important than ability.

—CHRISTINE DARDEN

Never walk into or out of a meeting without a clear agenda.

—MARY JANE RYAN

Many a woman has a 'to-do' list that resembles the phone book! Don't overdo your 'to-do' list. Keep it reasonable and keep it doable.

—LESLIE ROSSMAN

☺
22

Write out your problem on a piece of paper, stick the paper in a drawer, and close it. Do not allow yourself to look at or think about the list until the end of the week. By then, you may look at your problems differently and will have solutions.

—MICHELLE STRONG

I don't wait for moods. You accomplish nothing if you do that. Your mind must know it has got to get down to work.

—PEARL S .BUCK

☺
—
23

PLAN AND PREPARE

Look twice before you leap.

—CHARLOTTE BRONTË

The very best impromptu speeches are
the ones written well in advance.

—RUTH GORDON

What I've learned from fairy tales:
Invest in some good string rather than
breadcrumbs. That way, you can always find
the path back to the gingerbread house.

—WENDY ST. CHARLES

☺

24

Failing to plan is planning to fail.

—EFFIE JONES

If one asks for success and prepares
for failure, she will get the situation
she has prepared for.

—FLORENCE SCOVEL SHINN

Don't agonize. Organize.

—FLORYNCE KENNEDY

Plans are necessary to life and achievement
in any sphere. But they should never
overcome our powers of flexibility.

—DIXIE MARTIN

Lack of confidence is born from a
lack of preparation.

—SHANNON WILBURN

Luck is a matter of preparation
meeting opportunity.

—OPRAH WINFREY

☺
—
25

You had better live your best and act your
best and think your best today; for today is
the sure preparation for tomorrow and all
the other tomorrows that follow.

—HARRIET MARTINEAU

Winning is the science of being
totally prepared.

—GRACIE ALLEN

Preparation, I have often said, is rightly
two-thirds of any venture.

—AMELIA EARHART

DREAM ON!

☺

26

Fantasies are more than substitutes for
unpleasant reality; they are also dress
rehearsals, plans. All acts performed in the
world begin in the imagination.

—BARBARA GRIZZUTI HARRISON

What the world really needs is more love
and less paperwork.

—PEARL BAILEY

If we would only give, just once, the
same amount of reflection to what we
want to get out of life that we give to the
question of what to do with a two weeks'
vacation, we would be startled at the
aimless procession of our busy days.

—DOROTHY CANFIELD FISHER

I want to so order my life that its
impression, its impact, might always be
positive and spiritually constructive.

☺
—
27

—DOROTHY BROWN

For the happiest life, days
should be rigorously planned, nights
left open to chance.

—MIGNON MCLAUGHLIN

To stay ahead, you must have your next
idea waiting in the wings.

—ROSABETH MOSS KANTER

All the flowers of all the tomorrows
are in the seeds of today.

—PROVERB

Make big plans; aim high in hope and work,
remembering that a noble and logical plan
never dies, but long after we are gone will
be a living thing.

—LITA BANE

It's never too late—in fiction or
in life—to revise.

—NANCY THAYER

TAKE YOUR LIFE IN YOUR OWN HANDS

It's true that life's gifts come with responsibilities. When I don't feel like cleaning up my desk or my car or my house or my general existence, I try to remember the people who would be desperate to have all the things I take for granted.

—RACHEL CLARKSON

☺

29

You take your life in your own hands, and what happens? A terrible thing: no one to blame.

—ERICA JONG

Make decisions in a timely fashion—rarely does waiting improve the quality of the decision.

—ODETTE POLLAR

This is a wonderful world for women.
The richness, the hope, the promise of
life today…are exciting beyond belief.
Nonetheless, we need stout hearts and
strong characters; we need knowledge
and training; we need organized effort to
meet the future.

—BELLE S. SPAFFORD

When planning for a year, plant corn.

☺
—
30

When planning for a decade, plant trees.

When planning for life, train
and educate people.

—CHINESE PROVERB

I don't know that there are any shortcuts
to doing a good job.

—SANDRA DAY O'CONNOR

I was taught the way of progress is neither swift nor easy.

—MARIE CURIE

SOME HELPFUL HOW-TOS

I must govern the clock, not be governed by it.

—GOLDA MEIR

☺

31

If only everything were as easily organized as, say, my shoe collection. And even that can sometimes be a losing battle.

—SASHA MORROW

There are so many options, so much to do, so many demands on women. There is no point in taking one hour to do a ten-minute task, nor should we slap together an hour-worthy project in ten minutes.

—ELAINE CANNON

Arrange whatever
pieces come your way.

—VIRGINIA WOOLF

A team is more than a collection of people. It is a process of give and take.

—BARBARA GLACEL

Effective teamwork is all about making a good, well-balanced salad, not whipping individuals into a single batch of V8.

—SANDRA RICHARDSON

Take just a few minutes
each day to sort through any
miscellaneous papers on your desk at
home or the office, rather than letting
unorganized piles multiply and grow.

—GLADYS MORISSON

To achieve your dreams,
remember your ABC's:
Avoid negative sources, people, places,
things, and habits. Believe in yourself.
Consider things from every angle.

—WANDA HOPE CARTER

☺

33

Keep things as simple as possible…
nobody wants to reorganize their system
of reorganization!

—CASSIE LAWRENCE

If a problem has no solution,
it's not a problem, just a fact.

—BJ GALLAGHER

There are two ways of meeting difficulties.
You alter the difficulties or you alter
yourself to meet them.

—PHYLLIS BOTTOMED

☺

34

Adopt the highly effective SAW inbox
system: ["S" for] STAT (as in a hospital
emergency room) means "do it now!"
and is for urgent tasks with a deadline of
today. "A" stands for "as soon as possible"
and goes on your to-do list with doable
deadlines. "W" stands for "whenever" and
is only for ideas and wishes for the future.

—ROBERTA LEFFLER

I always say don't make plans,
make options.

—JENNIFER ANISTON

Get a three-ring binder with
pocketed dividers for receipts and user
manuals, and organize by need such as
"birthdays," "utility bills," "credit cards
and reports," "computer info," and most
importantly, "taxes"!

—NINA LESOWITZ

☺
—
35

One way to keep control over
the paper in your life is to get it back
in circulation. Do you have a stack of
magazines that you are almost done with?
Take a few moments to go through them,
and then pass them on to friends, a library,
a school, a hospital, or a charity thrift
shop. I have a magazine "trade" system set
up with some girlfriends!

—LILLIAN CRIST

The most successful people in the world break big tasks down into doable pieces. If you have a major goal that feels overwhelming to you—slice and dice it. One step at a time and the mountain is climbed—now, doesn't that feel great?

—DEENA PATEL-WINE

I make the most of all that comes and the least of all that goes.

—SARA TEASDALE

☺

Never rely just on your smartphone or a file on your computer to safely store your mailing addresses, numbers, and email addresses. Just one computer crash or loss of your smartphone can render you helpless if you lack backups, whether to the cloud, a hard copy, or thumb drives in safe remote locations!

—SUZANNA HARWELL

Less Can Truly Be More

You should only have possessions you really love;
don't let your things possess you. I have a neat-
looking "outbox" on my front porch that I fill during
the week with items I can take to the Reuse Center
at my neighborhood recycling location. As the days
go by, magazines, extra pots and pans, odd cups and
dishes, old electronics, and any things that no longer
have a place in my home go there. My partner and
I go there at least twice a month, and it simply feels
wonderful. The center has a lot of regulars, and we
are now recognized as purveyors of 100 percent
discount bounty, such as scented candles, barely-
worn scarves, office supplies, crockery, and superb
magazines, as we are a household of voracious
readers. I have seen amazing trades at the Reuse
Center, and I witnessed a musician sitting down and
playing a free sitar with virtuosity while a family with
young children got a sorely needed washing machine
and dryer. Moments like this remind me of a novel by
the visionary teacher and writer Starhawk; *The Fifth
Sacred Thing* depicts a future where people return to
a barter system and live harmoniously in community.

Take only what you need and share anything extra
with your own neighbors.

Chapter Two

Self-Care: Love Yourself
So You Can Love Your Life

Be kind to yourself, too. Make a commitment to yourself to refrain from negative self-talk. Be kind to yourself and focus on the traits you like rather than the ones you don't. The extremely wise Dawna Markova, the author of some of my favorite books, including *I Will Not Die an Unlived Life,* says, "Your soul remembers when you put yourself down; it imprints upon you. Never do this. Self-compassion is key to a life well-lived." How can you take better care of yourself?

You know the feeling too well: you're worn out. The rope you're dangling at the end of is frayed and about to snap. But you can't stop. Your to-do list is longer than the beginnings of that novel you've been working on, and every second that ticks by is gone forever. STOP! You're no good to anyone in this state—not to your boss, your best friends, your family, and most of all yourself.

In high school, I was a bit of an overachiever, wearing myself to the bone to get good grades and participate in every extracurricular activity I could. Overall I enjoyed it, but I remember waking up one morning and having my mother tell me I should stay home from school. I wasn't really sick, but I was exhausted. I didn't know what to make of it—most parents would punish their kids for trying to get out of going to school. But her lesson was partly about perspective. If I was sacrificing my health and my sanity for things that were meant to be fulfilling and fun, what was the point? And she knew better than I that some downtime would refresh me, and then I could hit the ground running the next day doing what I loved.

Naps. Walks. Quiet time. Meditation. Breathing. Daydreaming. Baths. A good book. Or maybe best of all, doing nothing. When's the last time you took a step back and really took a moment for yourself? It's about time. Here are a few famous quotes as well as some tried-and-true suggestions from ladies like you and me for taking good care of number one.

SLOW DOWN

If you realize too acutely
how valuable time is, you are too
paralyzed to do anything.

—KATHARINE BUTLER HATHAWAY

To achieve the impossible dream,
try going to sleep.

—JOAN KLEMPNER

☺
41

Like kids, adults need time-outs too, but
it's usually to keep from doing something
bad rather than as punishment.

—KATHY FREEMAN

A good rest is half the work.

—PROVERB

Relaxation is an art that has been made
very difficult to practice by the conditions
of modern civilization.

—ALANIS MORISSETTE

For fast-acting relief, try slowing down.

—LILY TOMLIN

Regardless of your religion, go inside a
local church, temple, or synagogue and
sit for a half an hour when there is no
service happening. Simply sit and enjoy the
company of your thoughts, the mellow
lighting, and the reflective atmosphere.

—JAY KHAN

If you don't take naps, take one!
Take a nap in the middle of the day when
you are unusually overwhelmed. Just doing
this once during an "off limits" time will
renew your sense of self and allow you to
stay on task the rest of the time!

—DONNA OLICKIN

Take a bath early in the morning, before
you begin your daily routine. Get up earlier
if you have to and immerse yourself in the
tub. You will have a relaxed day.

—POLLY PORTER

☺

43

Interrupt your daily routine
on a weekend by doing nothing;
it brings a fresh perspective.

—CAROL WISEMAN

LAUGH OUT LOUD

You grow up the day you have your
first real laugh at yourself.

—ETHEL BARRYMORE

Housework can't kill you,
but why take a chance?

—PHYLLIS DILLER

☺
—
44

Remember that thing they say about
stopping and counting to ten? It only
works if you're sane enough to count.

—ALEX PRESTON

I am woman! I am invincible!
I am pooped!

—BJ GALLAGHER

Insanity is my only means of relaxation.

—VARLA VENTURA

Read some young adult fiction—
a Nancy Drew book or anything by
Lemony Snicket. Get yourself out of the
busy adult world and remember what it
was like to get lost in a book.

—EVELYN VANDERMERE

☺
—

Here is the opposite of your "to-do" list
for work! Make an "I want to do this"
list. It can be as adventurous as possible,
anything you want to accomplish in
your life: plant a gorgeous garden, go to
Australia and surf, learn to play piano,
hang glide. Just by making the list, you are
helping your wild wishes come true!

—LOTTE WARNER

LEARN AND SHARE

Love the moment, and the
energy of that moment will spread
beyond all boundaries.

—SISTER CORITA KENT

Take up a new hobby you've always
been interested in. Learning a new skill
will make you feel productive, even if that
skill is only for your enjoyment.

—LAURA BAKER

Don't forget the simple
pleasures of your past. Recently
I remembered a favorite present from my
childhood, an origami kit. I bought myself
a new kit and was delighted to find that
making these tiny works of art can still
focus and clear my mind.

—MABLE EVANS

A potluck with friends may be a simple tradition, but it's one of the most fun and even rewarding to uphold.

—FLORENCE ALLEN

A change of scenery is often the easiest way to take time away from our everyday lives. Never underestimate the benefits of a simple day trip alone or with friends.

—REBECCA GLEESOB

☺

47

Museums are some of the best places to gain a bit of relaxation and perspective. You have to think about something besides your own problems when surrounded by the evidence of so much other reality.

—CANDICE LONG

Listen to music you like, and cultivate that interest actively—go to concerts, listen to CDs you have never heard at the store, and share your taste with friends. Music communicates to us on many different levels, and your favorite music tends to transport your mind to its favorite place.

—KIMBERLY LYNN DAVIS

☺
—
48

Develop your green thumb—even if you only have a couple of pots on your deck or fire escape. Learn all about plants online or at the local nursery, and add seasonal plants for spring and fall. Not only will you be creating beauty, you will be more in tune with nature and the seasons.

—RUTH BAXTER

Pets are great happiness boosters.
The companionship, love, and
entertainment a pet provides is for
many people as significant as any human
relationship. Medical researchers have
even discovered that petting your pets
reduces blood pressure!

—SHELLY STRONG

Grab your wild friends and have a
clothing swap. Set aside clothes or
accessories you don't wear, gather with
friends who've done the same, and begin
a fair trade. Spice up your wardrobe
without spending money!

—DEE LOGAN

☺

49

LET IT GO

Forget the past and live
the present hour.

—SARAH KNOWLES BOLTON

The jump is so frightening between
where I am and where I want to be…
because of all I may become, I will close
my eyes and leap!

—MARY ANNE RADMACHER

Worry does not empty tomorrow of its
sorrow; it empties today of its strength.

—CORRIE TEN BOOM

You can always find reasons to work.
There will always be one more thing to
do. But when people don't take time out,
they stop being productive. They stop
being happy, and that affects the morale of
everyone around them.

—CARISA BIANCHI

Wrinkles are called worry
lines for a reason.

☺
—JANICE THOMPSON

Stress is an ignorant state. It believes that
everything is an emergency. Nothing is
that important.

—NATALIE GOLDBERG

Tension is who you think you should be.
Relaxation is who you are.

—CHINESE PROVERB

If only we'd stop trying to be happy we'd
have a pretty good time.

—EDITH WHARTON

Lose track of time—on a weekend,
declare it a "no watch" weekend!
Notice how much more relaxed you
will be if you are not always looking at
your watch. Ahhhh.

—JULIE HENNESSY

☺

52

SIMPLIFY

Life isn't a matter of milestones
but of moments.

—ROSE FITZGERALD KENNEDY

There is no need to go to India or
anywhere else to find peace. You will find
that deep place of silence right in your
room, your garden, or even your bathtub.

—ELISABETH KÜBLER-ROSS

To sit in the shade on a fine
day and look upon verdure is the most
perfect refreshment.

—JANE AUSTEN

☺
—
53

The sound of birds stops the
noise in my mind.

—CARLY SIMON

Sometimes the most important thing
in a whole day is the rest we take between
two long breaths, or the turning inwards
in prayer for five short minutes.

—ETTY HILLESUM

Like water which can clearly mirror
the sky and the trees only so long as its
surface is undisturbed, the mind can only
reflect the true image of the Self when it
is tranquil and wholly relaxed.

—INDRA DEVI

If you can attain repose and calm, believe
that you have seized happiness.

—JULIE-JEANNE-ÉLÉONORE
DE LESPINASSE

To instantaneously relax, slowly take four
deep inhales and exhales. Just focus on
your breath and slowly count to three as
you breathe.

—JEAN MCINTYRE

Turn off the television and the radio in
your car, office, and home for one full day.
Allow yourself to listen to the silence.

—VICTORIA MARTUCCI

One way to really relax is with a
warm mug of herbal tea—chamomile
is one of the most relaxing of all, while
peppermint both stimulates and calms.
An orange and rose hip tea is good for
unwinding and also adds a healthy
dose of vitamin C, too!

—ANALEYAH NORTH

Working in the garden gives me something
beyond the enjoyment of senses. It gives
me a profound sense of inner peace.

—RUTH STOUT

☺

55

CREATE CALM

Taking time for yourself should never be
seen as a burden. Not on you, and not on
anyone else.

—ELIZABETH FRANKLIN

People tell you to take care of yourself like it's an easy thing. It's not. It's a very hard thing sometimes, but there's no shame in making the effort.

—FAITH WALKER

Daily walks are one of my best discoveries. It's just about the only thing I can do for forty-five minutes without being interrupted.

☺

56

—FREIDA RAMONE

Take some time for yourself every single day. Even if it's just five minutes. Even if you have to lock the door.

—CASSIDY SNOW

Take a walk on your lunch hour!

—DEBRA POBLETE

It may be a cliché, but there often is
nothing better than preparing something
special to eat. Not for your family or your
friends, just for you.

—FRANCINE LOVETT

Designate one day a month as
Retreat Day. Turn off your phones, radio,
television, and computer. Read. Cook
yummy food. Sit in silence. Enjoy!

☺

—DREW BARRYMORE

Give yourself flowers—and really
do it! The longest lasting blooms are
sunflowers, Peruvian lilies, and dahlias. Most
importantly, getting the flowers will bring
the biggest smile to your face.

—ELISE MARIE COLLINS

After washing your hair, allow it to dry naturally in the sun.

—MADELEINE SOMERVILLE

Buy yourself a new loofah, a back brush, or a new washcloth and body wash with lavender essential oil. Use it!

—FRAN PETERSON

Take yourself out to dinner.

—STACY LEVINE

☺

58

Get a life! People who excel have a life outside of work, which makes them happier, and therefore, more efficient!

—PAYTON ROBINSON

Only when one is connected to one's own core is one connected to others. And for me, the core, the inner spring, can be best refound through solitude.

—ANNE MORROW LINDBERGH

If you're usually surrounded by people, spend a day all by yourself and enjoy the solitude—and the deliciousness—of your own company.

—CYNTHIA MACGREGOR

☺

Rewire Your Brain to Be More Positive

Neuropsychiatrist David Amen, MD, posits that thoughts carry physical properties and that the properties of negative thoughts can be detrimental to your leading a healthy, happy life. To overturn these negative effects, he prescribes thinking more positively, maintaining that by doing so, you can change the way your brain works and in turn change your life for the better.

Chapter Three

Express Yourself Through Your Personal Style

The essence of your style is all you. It sounds obvious, even silly. But how often do we flip through a magazine or look at others on the street and long to have some other woman's wardrobe, body, or charisma? The best make it look effortless, but we know it rarely is. The great thing about true style is that it stands on its own, and you don't have to judge or envy anyone else to get it, *because it's already yours.* Every outfit you admire, every color that lights up your face, every pair of shoes you flip for—they all reflect you at your best, ready to take on the world.

My best friend claims that whenever she's going through a major transformation—being fired or quitting a job, the end of a relationship, or a move—she buys one thing that seems outlandish for the circumstances. Something she may feel she can't quite afford, but that she absolutely loves and will treasure for a long time. She calls it her I'll-never-[work/be happy/fall in love]-again dress, and considers it a kind of reverse psychology good luck charm. The thinking goes that if she's all washed up, at least she has this one last beautiful thing to remember as she wallows in her misery. Of course, she's not one to wallow. And I think the true purpose is to force herself back into the game by embracing beauty in her own way and on her own terms. It cheers her right up to tote around a new bag or get compliments on an inspired new 'do. And let me tell you, it works for her…she's never been down in the dumps for long (and even if she was, she sure wouldn't look it.)

After conducting an informal poll of the most stylish women I know, I've put together the 1-2-3 rules. (And of course, the best of the best know how to outdo themselves by breaking every rule.)

☺
—
62

Simplicity is the key—especially on a budget. Clean lines, strong colors, no fuss.

Always feel comfortable in your clothes—if you love the way it looks on the hanger but feel funny every time you put it on, it goes right into the clothes swap pile.

Quality over quantity—for the price of a lot of cheap stuff that wears out in one season, buy one great thing you'll have forever.

EXPRESS YOUR
INNER BEAUTY

I think your whole life shows in your face
and you should be proud of that.

—LAUREN BACALL

Style may be on the surface, but you can
be deep and still have some.

—CLARISSA GOUGH

☺

63

Looking for a new sense of style? Try a
new sense of self first. It's cheaper, and you
won't have to get rid of the impulse buys.

—RHONDA BRADFORD

Kindness is always fashionable.

—AMELIA BARR

Fashion is not something that exists in dresses only. Fashion is in the sky, in the street, fashion has to do with ideas, the way we live, what is happening.

—COCO CHANEL

Fashion can be bought. Style one must possess.

—EDNA WOOLMAN CHASE

☺

Beauty is how you feel inside, and it reflects in your eyes. It is not something physical.

—SOPHIA LOREN

Fashions are always changing, but our friendships will never go out of style.

—REEDA JOSEPH

Style is based on who you are.

—ISABELLA ROSSELLINI

What about saying,
"This is how I look, and I'm beautiful and
I'm strong." You're not going to be what
everybody loves. But you have to love
yourself. Making the decision to do that is
something you can actually do.

—AMY SCHUMER

☺
—
65

Of all the things you wear, your expression
is the most important.

—JANET LANE

How many cares one loses when
one decides not to be something but
to be someone.

—COCO CHANEL

There is no cosmetic for
beauty like happiness.

—MARIA MITCHELL

SHOW YOUR SASS

If the shoe fits, it's too expensive.

—ADRIENNE GUSOFF

If high heels were so wonderful,
men would be wearing them.

—SUE GRAFTON

I base my fashion taste on
what doesn't itch.

—GILDA RADNER

We are entitled to wear cowboy
boots to our own revolution.

—NAOMI WOLF

Some women hold up dresses that are
so ugly, and they always say the same
thing: 'This looks much better on.'
On what? On fire?

—RITA RUDNER

The only rule is don't be boring…
Life is too short to blend in.

—PARIS HILTON

Give a girl the correct footwear and she
can conquer the world.

—BETTE MIDLER

I'm not offended by all the dumb blonde
jokes because I know I'm not dumb.
I also know I'm not blonde.

—DOLLY PARTON

67

Dear, NEVER forget one little point: It's MY business. You just work here.

—ELIZABETH ARDEN
(in a note to her husband)

I'm a big woman. I need big hair.

—ARETHA FRANKLIN

I wouldn't say I invented tacky, but I definitely brought it to its present high popularity.

—BETTE MIDLER

☺
—
68

SHOP 'TIL YOU DROP, PAMPER 'TIL YOU'RE POOPED

I would rather shop than eat!

—WALLIS SIMPSON

I feel sexy when I get out of the tub—
your skin is fresh and you've put up your
hair without looking.

—SHANIA TWAIN

She had the loaded handbag of
someone who camps out and seldom
goes home, or who imagines life must
be full of emergencies.

—MAVIS GALLANT

I love color and I love to dress
like a woman.

—LISA GUERRERO

I don't go out without makeup.
I'm a woman, you know.

—SHAKIRA

☺

69

There are no ugly women,
only lazy ones.

—HELENA RUBINSTEIN

I will buy any crème, cosmetic, or elixir
from a woman with a European accent.

—ERMA BOMBECK

Going hungry never bothered me—
it was having no clothes!

—CHER

Every best-dressed woman keeps some
of her gowns for years. She's learned
that fashion-wisdom is compounded of
knowledge, taste, confidence, and poise.

—LORETTA YOUNG

You'd be surprised how much it costs to look this cheap.

—DOLLY PARTON

I always say shopping is cheaper than a psychiatrist.

—TAMMY FAYE MESSNER

The only thing that separates us from the animals is our ability to accessorize.

—OLYMPIA DUKAKIS

☺

71

Paint your nails in two tones—next time you get a French manicure, ask for lime green and pink, or red and gold, or black with orange tips! Get creative!

—OLIVIA LAMONDE

For your next office holiday party
or power lunch, go vintage! Many higher-
end vintage clothing stores sell dresses,
suits, and blouses in like-new condition
at a fraction of the cost of new designer
clothing. These items are usually high
quality and add flair to your wardrobe.
Vintage clothing creates a classic
and unique look.

—TRINA ROBBINS

☺

Use your favorite lotion in your hair!
It tames the frizzies and
scents your hair beautifully!

—ALICE MARY ALVREZ

A purse with panache is a great way to
update your wardrobe. Invest in four
(practical) purses you absolutely love and
alternate them on a regular basis. For a
quick change of purses, keep your wallet,
cell phone, keys, and favorite lipstick in a
small makeup bag that can be transferred
at the drop of a hat!

— LIZA MINELLI

Jewelry is a quick and great way to
add some pizzazz to your outfit;
try sporting your favorite earrings
and a dazzling necklace. Once a year,
treat yourself and get all your jewelry
professionally cleaned—your gems will
sparkle like new!

—CHER

I take Him shopping with me. I say,
"Okay, Jesus, help me find a bargain."

—TAMMY FAYE MESSNER

☺
—
73

Forget diamonds, a girl's best friend
is the perfect-fitting dress!

—AMANDA FORD

Buy a collection of essential oils and make
your own fragrances and blends. Start
with the basics, like lavender, orange, and
mint, and expand as you experiment. You
can customize your sheets and laundry
soap with your new scent. You can even
scent your household cleaner by adding
a few drops of lavender oil! Create your
own signature scent!

—RHIANNON MAHONEY

OWNING YOURSELF

Nothing makes a woman more beautiful
than the belief that she is beautiful.

—SOPHIA LOREN

We have to have faith in ourselves.
I have never met a woman who, deep
down in her core, really believes she has
great legs. And if she suspects that she
might have great legs, then she's convinced
that she has a shrill voice and no neck.

—CYNTHIA HEIMEL

Fashion trends may not last forever,
but the photos will.

—ALICE TURNER

75

Even the most beautiful couture looks
shabby if you can't hold your head high
and strike a good pose.

—SANDRA COOR

I represent more the healthy, happy, curvy, strong woman. And that sounds much healthier to me than being eighty pounds and skinny as a bean.

—HEIDI KLUM

Toughness doesn't have to come in a pinstripe suit.

—SENATOR DIANNE FEINSTEIN

Get really dressed up for work one day for no other reason than just "putting your best foot forward," in your best earrings, a stunning suit, or a pretty dress, and obviously, your favorite dressy shoes.

—LARA STARR

We've come a long way. Power dressing now is designed to let the woman inside us come through.

—DONNA KARAN

While clothes may not make the woman,
they certainly have a strong effect on her
self-confidence—which, I believe, does
make the woman.

—MARY KAY ASH

VAMP IT UP

Being a sex symbol has to do with an
attitude, not looks. Most men think it's
looks, most women know otherwise.

—KATHLEEN TURNER

A woman is no older than she looks.

—ELIZABETH TAYLOR

77

It's no secret that I love a powerful yet slightly fragile woman such as Garbo, Lillian Gish, Bette Davis…that's where I get my inspirations from.

—SIOBHAN FAHEY

Glamour is what I sell; it's my stock in trade.

—MARLENE DIETRICH

There are various orders of beauty, causing men to make fools of themselves in various styles.

—GEORGE ELIOT

Wear red! It is flattering on everyone and a great alternative to black.

—RIRI

I don't know who invented high heels, but all women owe him a lot.

—MARILYN MONROE

Sex appeal is fifty percent what you've got and fifty percent what people think you've got.

—SOPHIA LOREN

Scratch most feminists and underneath there is a woman who longs to be a sex object. The difference is that is not all she wants to be.

—BETTY ROLLIN

☺

79

BRAINY IS BEAUTIFUL

Any girl can be glamorous. All you have to do is stand still and look stupid.

—HEDY LAMARR

You don't have to signal a social conscience by looking like a frump. Lace knickers won't hasten the holocaust…and a mild interest in the length of hemlines doesn't necessarily disqualify you from reading Das Kapital and agreeing with every word.

—ELIZABETH BIBESCO

You get out of fashion what you put into it.

—LORETTA YOUNG

I'm not interested in age. People who tell me their age are silly. You're as old as you feel.

—ELIZABETH ARDEN

I'm not obsessed by how I look or with being reed thin, but I do think that as a woman in my fifties, I have forty years ahead. Looking after yourself goes hand in hand with looking good.

—LINDA EVANS

If truth is beauty, how come no one has her hair done in a library?

—LILY TOMLIN

☺

81

Don't buy clothes at the last minute, and try to decide what you are going to wear to an important meeting or date a night in advance. If possible, try the outfit on a few nights before the event and wear it around your apartment to make sure you are comfortable.

—KATY PERRY

Elegance is refusal.

—COCO CHANEL

I began wearing hats as a young lawyer
because it helped me to establish
my professional identity. Before that,
whenever I was at a meeting, someone
would ask me to get the coffee—they
assumed I was a secretary.

—CONGRESSWOMAN BELLA ABZUG

Give Your Old Clothes a Promotion

Donate your unworn professional clothing to http://www.dressforsuccess.org/. This organization promotes economic independence for disadvantaged women by providing them with clothing they can wear to job interviews and to their place of work.

☺

Chapter Four

With a Little Help from Your Friends, Family, and a Mentor or Two

We need friends. What would life be without them? Lonely, for one. What does friendship mean? Friends touch our hearts, enrich our lives, bolster our hopes, and forgive our ugly moments. They offer an outside perspective. They know us better than we know ourselves. True friends give sound advice and tell us the truth, even when it hurts. They listen to our woes and our joys and stand by us when no one else will.

The girl you met on the first day of second grade. Your mentor at work. The great aunt who swoops into town to take you to a fancy lunch just when you need it most. Friends who share passions or just live down the street. Through friends we are connected by degrees to every other human being on the planet, so friendship really does bind the world together.

Even better, friends are free of charge. There are no legal ties to friendship, no contracts, usually not even a blood relationship (though being friends with your mom, sisters, or cousins has its own rewards.) They are the people we choose to bond with—and they become our second family. Sometimes they're way more sane and likable than the one we're born into.

What about the dreaded fight with your best friend? It leaves you heartsick, and if you can't patch it up, you'll feel the ache for a long time to come. Take my advice and do what you can to make it better. Life's too short to live with regrets, and way too short to live without good friends. When I look back on fights with friends, I cringe at my own silly pride.

☺
—
86

The only thing better than having a friend is *being* a friend. With friendship comes responsibility—the challenge of looking outside ourselves and investing in someone else's happiness. The greatest reward of friendship is helping your friends become their best in every way.

We don't always have to donate time and energy to other parts of the world. Sometimes help is needed much close to home. Is a parent, sibling, spouse, or friend having a difficult time? Let them experience that loving feeling and help lift their spirits. Invite them to coffee or to dinner, surprise them with a simple gift, and take them somewhere they like. Lean forward and listen closely. Just hear them out, because listening is an act of love.

THE WONDER OF FRIENDS

My true friends have always given me that
supreme proof of devotion, a spontaneous
aversion to the man I loved.

—COLETTE

Time spent with friends is healing because
we don't perceive it as time. We just are.

—GRACE MORTON

☺

87

Trouble is like a sieve through which we
sift our acquaintances. Those too big to
pass through are our friends.

—ARLENE FRANCIS

To be rich in friends is to be
poor in nothing.

—LILIAN WHITING

Each friend represents a world in us, a
world possibly not born until they arrive,
and it is only by this meeting that a new
world is born.

—ANAÏS NIN

A friend is someone who knows all about
you and loves you anyway!

—NANCY LAUREN FISH

☺
—
88

Though friendship is not quick to burn,
it is explosive stuff.

—MAY SARTON

Walking with a friend in the dark is better
than walking alone in the light.

—HELEN KELLER

The friend who holds your hand and says
the wrong thing is made of dearer stuff
than the one who stays away.

—BARBARA KINGSOLVER

Happiness is the comfortable
companionship of friends.

—PAM BROWN

Animals are such agreeable friends, they
ask no questions, they pass no criticism.

—GEORGE ELIOT

What's really important in life—
friends, friends, friends.

—FANNIE FLAGG

A friend is someone who reaches for your
hand but touches your heart.

—KATHLEEN FROVE

Friends are like angels following you
through life.

—MARY ELLEN

My friends are my estate.

—EMILY DICKINSON

Never doubt that a small group of
dedicated people can make a difference.
Indeed, it is the only thing that ever has.

—MARGARET MEAD

Life's truest happiness is found in
friendships we make along the way.

—LAUREN RUIZ

A friend is someone who knows the song
in your heart and can sing it back to you
when you have forgotten the words.

—DONNA ROBERTS

WHAT WOULD WE DO WITHOUT THEM?

Loneliness is the most terrible poverty.

—MOTHER TERESA

☺
—
91

The only true disability would be to go
through life without friendship.

—LAURA FORTH

A friend is like a four-leaf clover, hard to
find but lucky to have.

—SAMANTHA ROSALES

It seems to me that trying to live without
friends is like milking a bear to get cream
for your morning coffee. It is a whole lot
of trouble, and then not worth much after
you get it.

—ZORA NEALE HURSTON

CARE AND FEEDING

A friendship can weather most things
and thrive in thin soil; but it needs a little
mulch of letters and phone calls and small,
silly presents every so often—just to save
it from drying out completely.

—PAM BROWN

Plant a seed of friendship—reap a
bouquet of happiness.

—LOIS L. KAUFMAN

There may not be a recipe for friendship,
but that doesn't mean there are no rules.

—BLANCHE HARDING

They call it "making friends" for a reason.
It takes effort, and the right ingredients.

—SANDRA GARRETT

A new friendship is like an
unripened fruit—it may become either
an orange or a lemon.

☺
—
93

—EMMA STACEY

If you judge people, you have
no time to love them.

—MOTHER TERESA

Silences make the real conversations between friends. Not the saying but the never needing to say is what counts.

—MARGARET LEE RUNBECK

It takes a lot of courage to show your dreams to someone else.

—ERMA BOMBECK

The sharing of joy, whether physical, emotional, psychic, or intellectual, forms a bridge between the sharers which can be the basis for understanding much of what is not shared between them, and lessens the threat of their difference.

—AUDRE LORDE

The only thing to do is to hug one's friends tight and do one's job.

—EDITH WHARTON

For women, talk is the glue that holds
relationships together; it creates
connections between people and a sense
of community.

—DEBORAH FARMER

Count your joys instead of your woes;
count your friends instead of your foes.

—IRISH PROVERB

☺
95

Strangers are just friends
waiting to happen!

—WENDY WENTWORTH

Make new friends and keep the old; one is
silver and the other is gold.

—GIRL SCOUT MOTTO

We are each other's
magnitude and bond.

—GWENDOLYN BROOKS

"Stay" is a charming word in a
friend's vocabulary.

—LOUISA MAY ALCOTT

CONNECTION

Friendship is the golden ribbon that ties
the world together.

—KRISTINA KENTIGLAN

I am treating you as my friend, asking you
to share my present minuses in the hope I
can ask you to share my future pluses.

—KATHERINE MANSFIELD

Two may talk together
under the same roof for many years, yet
never really meet; and two others at first
speech are old friends.

—MARY CATHERWOOD

Though our communication wanes at
times of absence, I'm aware of a strength
that emanates in the background.

—CLAUDETTE RENNER

☺
—
97

In loneliness, in sickness,
in confusion—the mere knowledge of
friendship makes it possible to endure,
even if the friend is powerless to help.
It is enough that they exist.

—PAM BROWN

Ah, how good it feels…
the hand of an old friend.

—MARY ENGELBREIT

I don't want to lose this happy space
where I have found someone who is smart
and easy and doesn't bother to check her
diary when we arrange to meet.

—JEANETTE WINTERSON

There is magic in long-distance
friendships. They let you relate to other
human beings in a way that goes beyond
being physically together and is often
more profound.

—DIANA CORTES

There is no distance too great between
friends, for love gives wings to the heart.

—ELIZABETH E. KOEHLER

Some people go to priests;
others to poetry; I to my friends.

—VIRGINIA WOOLF

GIVING

You never lose by loving.
You always lose by holding back.

—BARBARA DE ANGELIS

☺
—
99

If we would build on a sure foundation in
friendship, we must love friends for their
own sake rather than our own.

—CHARLOTTE BRONTË

The finest kind of friendship is between
two people who expect a great deal of
each other, but never ask it.

—SYLVIA BREMER

I don't get women who pick fights
with their friends. It's not like you get to
kiss and make up afterwards. Play those
games with your lover if you have to, but
don't toy with a good friendship.

—MARCIA BOND

We all need friends with
whom we can speak of our deepest
concerns, and who do not fear to speak
the truth in love to us.

—REV. MARGARET GUENTHER

☺
—
100

Constant use will not wear ragged
the fabric of friendship.

—DOROTHY PARKER

The best time to make friends is
before you need them.

—ETHEL BARRYMORE

It's important to our friends to
believe that we are unreservedly frank
with them, and important to the friendship
that we are not.

—MIGNON MCLAUGHLIN

Send a thank you note to a good friend,
a relative, or coworker "just because" and
let them know what you appreciate about
them. This "attitude of gratitude" will take
you far in your life and will come back to
you many times over.

—MARY JANE RYAN

A real friend is one who walks in when
the rest of the world walks out.

—JENNIFER ANISTON

☺
—
101

Friendship with oneself is all-important,
because without it, one cannot be friends
with anybody else in the world.

—ELEANOR ROOSEVELT

I've always believed that one
woman's success can only help another
woman's success.

—GLORIA VANDERBILT

☺
102

We cherish our friends not
for their ability to amuse us, but for ours
to amuse them.

—EVELYN WAUGH

A good friend brings out the
best in everybody!

—MIMI COOKE

GROWING

The most beautiful discovery that true
friends can make is that you can grow
separately without growing apart.

—ELIZABETH FOLEY

All you'll get from strangers is surface
pleasantry or indifference. Only someone
who loves you will criticize you.

—JUDITH CRIST

☺
—
103

Four be the things I am wiser to know:
Idleness, sorrow, a friend, and a foe.

—DOROTHY PARKER

No person is your friend who demands
your silence, or denies your right to grow.

—ALICE WALKER

Parents start you off on life but friends
get you through it.

—DEE CHOU

I can trust my friends. These people force
me to examine, encourage me to grow.

—CHER

It is the friends you call up at
4 a.m. that matter.

☺
—

104

—MARLENE DIETRICH

Don't Be Judgmental;
Be Kind Just Because You Can

It's easy to judge others for their actions and take for granted those we love or those we meet in chance encounters. We sometimes get so caught up in our busy-ness that we forget others are busy too, they have rough days just like us, and they benefit from our kindnesses just as we do from theirs. Go out of your way to smile at strangers, say good morning, say thank you, give a compliment, and listen attentively to someone who needs your ear. Do it because you can, because it feels great, because it makes someone else feel good. Don't worry about a subsequent thank you; let a thank you be a beautiful perk, rather than an expectation.

Chapter Five

Treat Yourself Well:
Hard Work Deserves Reward

Think about how you can create little moments of happiness for others. Helping a friend plant her garden, buying an extra coffee for your coworker, paying the toll for the car behind you on the bridge, even taking your kids to a movie. All those little things can add up to BIG joy.

☺

Now apply that same thinking to yourself. Try soaking your feet, having a facial, treating yourself to dinner. Or even going beyond the mundane to splurge on a real vacation. Vacations are really important. A weekend on the beach can erase a month of city tension. And you can learn new things, work through problems, and strengthen relationships at turbo speeds in the parallel vacation universe. Go on, give it a try. Make a commitment to pamper yourself a little on the way to realizing your dreams.

YOU DESERVE IT

I have an everyday religion that
works for me. Love yourself first,
and everything else falls into line.

—LUCILLE BALL

To be a saint does not exclude fine
dresses nor a beautiful house.

☺
—
108

—KATHERINE TYNAN HINKSON

Chocolate has iron in it.
Surely that's why I like it so much.

—ERIN YOUNG

Birds sing after a storm; why shouldn't
people feel as free to delight in whatever
remains to them?

—ROSE FITZGERALD KENNEDY

As women, we are taught to fear our own desires much more than men. Anything we want, we are told, should be considered suspect….While it is wise to carefully examine what we want and what we need, wanting in itself should not be so feared.

—ALANA PRICE

If you always do what interests you, then at least one person is pleased.

—KATHARINE HEPBURN

☺
109

I have low self-esteem, but I express it the healthy way…by eating a box of Double-Stuff Oreos.

—MIRANDA (CYNTHIA NIXON),
Sex And The City

Money earned with pains should be spent with pleasure.

—CHINESE PROVERB

Pleasure that isn't paid for is as insipid as everything else that's free.

—ANITA LOOS

We can each define ambition and progress for ourselves. The goal is to work toward a world where expectations are not set by the stereotypes that hold us back, but by our personal passion, talents, and interests.

—SHERYL SANDBERG

☺

Without leaps of imagination or dreaming, we lose the excitement of possibilities. Dreaming, after all, is a form of planning.

—GLORIA STEINEM

DON'T WAIT

Life is uncertain. Eat desserts first.

—MARGIE LAPANJA

Our best gifts to ourselves may be few,
but that doesn't mean they have to
be far between.

—DELILAH CARR

☺
—
111

Seize the moment. Remember all
those women on the Titanic who waved
off the dessert cart.

—ERMA BOMBECK

You have to treat yourself every once in a
while, get to the fun stuff!

—HEIDI KLUM

The essence of pleasure is spontaneity.

—GERMAINE GREER

While many fantasies are best left
to the realm of the imagination, some
must be fulfilled if we are to be healthy,
growing individuals.

—AMANDA BENNET

☺

112

It is only possible to live happily-ever-after
on a day-to-day basis.

—MARGARET THATCHER

Never let your senses become dulled to
your life. They are your only links to the
world around you.

—JUSTINE THOREAU

This very moment is a seed
from which the flowers of tomorrow's
happiness grow.

—MARGARET LINDSEY

I believe in dreams, not just the kind we
have at night. I think that if we hang on to
them, they come true.

—DANIELLE STEEL

☺

113

Life is to be lived.

—KATHARINE HEPBURN

THE BEST THINGS IN LIFE
(AND SOME ARE FREE!)

I love luxury. And luxury lies not in
richness and ornateness but in the
absence of vulgarity.

—COCO CHANEL

Food is, delightfully, an area of
licensed sensuality, of physical delight,
which will, with luck and enduring taste
buds, last our life long.

—ANTONIA TILL

No entertainment is so cheap as reading,
nor any pleasure so lasting.

—MARY WORTLEY MONTAGU

☺

Fragrance can have a great effect on
our well-being, triggering happy memories
or unlocking our sensuality. Indulge in
some new oils, candles, or perfumes and
enjoy the results.

—NANCY KLINE

Call your best friend for no other
reason than just to catch up—indulge
in laughs, a quick catch-up, and the beauty
of friendship.

—LEIGH STONE

Music melts all the separate parts of our
bodies together.

—ANAÏS NIN

☺

OVER-THE-TOP INDULGENCE

It is impossible to overdo luxury.

—FRENCH PROVERB

We owe something to extravagance,
for thrift and adventure seldom go
hand in hand.

—JENNIE JEROME CHURCHILL

We must deprogram ourselves from the
belief that all indulgence is sinful.
Only excess is sinful.

—YOLANDA BROOKS

Life itself is the proper binge.

—JULIA CHILD

Art may be one of humankind's
biggest indulgences, but it's also basic
to our survival.

—MARYA WHITBECK

☺
—
116

Take care of the luxuries and the
necessities will take care of themselves.

—DOROTHY PARKER

To be overcome by the fragrance of
flowers is a delectable form of defeat.

—BEVERLY NICHOLS

TRY THIS

Eat outdoors. Enjoy an entire dinner
service in the backyard, or even on a small
balcony. If you don't have outdoor space,
head for the park. Use real silverware and
cloth napkins. Indulge!

—BELINDA DECAMP

Go for a walk in the rain.

—CYNTHIA MACGREGOR

☺

Make your bedroom a sensuous place for
refuge. Do your work somewhere else in
the house, and decorate with your favorite
colors and textures. It should be your
own special luxurious hideaway.

—KATHRYN LAMONT

Those who allow their day to pass by
without practicing generosity and enjoying
life's pleasures are like a blacksmith's
bellows: they breathe but do not live.

—PROVERB

When I thought I had seen it all,
I went for a ride in a hot air balloon. The
perspective renewed my sense of awe in
the world around me!

—PATTY HELMS

☺

118

Treat yourself to the sweet joy of
dreaming of beautiful things, a fabulous
job, a fulfilling relationship.

—JUDY FORD

Every time I get a paycheck, I take a few dollars from it and set them aside for myself. That way, I have a small fund for when I see that perfect pair of pumps, without having to pump my credit card.

—BETHANY FLEMING

Live nutty. Just occasionally. Just once in a while and see what happens. It brightens up your day.

—PAT GURITZ

☺

119

Whip up an easy batch of your own bath salts. Inexpensive Epsom salts from the pharmacy will do; for a real treat, mix them with sea salt. Toss them into a Ziploc bag and add a few drops of your favorite essential oil. Shake the baggie until the oil is distributed throughout, and then draw yourself a hot bath!

—FRANCIS L. BAG

Give yourself a scalp massage the next
time you wash your hair.

—DOLLY WHITTIER

Paint a room in your house or
apartment a color you love—fiery red,
bright blue, or lavishing lavender—and
enjoy the new ambiance.

—CERRIDWEN GREENLEAF

☺

120

Give yourself a break from cooking
tonight; instead, have dinner delivered and
enjoy your additional free time.

—JENNIFER LEWIS

Far away there in the sunshine are
my highest aspirations. I may not reach
them, but I can look up and see their
beauty, believe in them, and try to follow
where they lead.

—LOUISA MAY ALCOTT

SIMPLE PLEASURES

I have a simple philosophy:
Fill what's empty. Empty what's full.
Scratch where it itches.

—ALICE ROOSEVELT LONGWORTH

It's an indulgence to sit in a room and
discuss your beliefs as if they were a
juicy piece of gossip.

—LILLIAN HELLMAN

☺

121

Life in the country teaches one
that the really stimulating things are
the quiet, natural things.…The scent of
grass is more luxurious than the most
expensive perfume.

—BEVERLEY NICHOLS

Real luxury is time and opportunity
to read for pleasure.

—JANE BRODY

To me, a lush carpet of pine needles or
spongy grass is more welcome than the
most luxurious Persian rug.

—HELEN KELLER

☺

122

Start a garden and plant it with only
your favorite seasonal flowers. Grow your
own special outdoor retreat, even if it's
only a window box.

—CYNTHIA KINGSTON

What do I want to take home from my
summer vacation? Time. The wonderful
luxury of being at rest. The days when you
shut down…and let life simply wander.

—ELLEN GOODMAN

Buying is a profound pleasure.

—SIMONE DE BEAUVOIR

If one could be friendly with women, what a pleasure—the relationship so secret and private compared with relations with men.

—VIRGINIA WOOLF

Museums and art stores are also sources of pleasure and inspiration…it is true that I derive genuine pleasure from touch.

—HELEN KELLER

God made all pleasures innocent.

—CAROLINE NORTON

☺

No Strings Attached

Write down the things that someone has given you, with no strings attached, for which you are grateful. It can be an old sofa, some sound advice, or a lift to the airport. Now list ten things that you would like to give someone yourself, and see how many of those things you can cross off in a week.

Examples:

Drive a friend to the airport

Carry groceries for an elder

Babysit for a relative

Buy a friend a cup of coffee

Volunteer at a soup kitchen

Weed an older neighbor's garden

Take fresh-out-of-the-oven doughnuts to a senior center and hang out

Chapter Six

Living Your Best Life Every Day

Take stock of your day-to-day life. Are you giving to others in your community, or are things a little out of balance where your work and your immediate family get 99 percent of what you offer the world? You can change that in one day by reconnecting to your dreams. What were your dreams when you were a child? We're all striving to make the most of what we've got; we all want better lives. But sometimes this desire becomes twisted, and we start to think that if only we had more money, or different circumstances, or just a little greener grass, that our lives would be perfect. Well, I am here to attest that perfect is boring—and life should be anything but boring. And while more and better stuff might be fun for a while, the real fun starts when we embrace the intangibles. The ingredients of a well-lived life are yours for the choosing: openness, strength, courage, dignity, responsibility, passion, positivity, energy, beauty, and whatever else you fancy.

It's time to take control of your destiny. Time to merge your inner child's enthusiasm with your adult experience. Believe you can live beyond your wildest dreams, voice your desires and act on them, and reap the benefits of a life lived to the hilt!

Uncover Your Soul's Purpose

When we are on track, living close to the things we deem important—the things we value—we feel happier. This isn't flash happiness, it isn't the kind that lasts for a few minutes when we get a new toy or enjoy a concert. This is the kind that lingers in the background of our lives, the kind that, even in moments of sadness or frustration, never completely disappears, because if we are living a values-based life, we are also living with meaning and purpose.

Polly Campbell

A bird doesn't sing because it has an
answer, it sings because it has a song.

—MAYA ANGELOU

The most important thing you will ever
do is become who you were meant to be.
Blossom into yourself.

—LISA HAMMOND

Invest in the human soul. Who knows,
it might be a diamond in the rough.

—MARY MCLEOD BETHUNE

☺

129

Life is what we make it, always has been,
always will be.

—GRANDMA MOSES

Don't be afraid your life will end; be afraid
that it will never begin.

—GRACE HANSEN

You don't get to choose how you're going to die, or when. You can only decide how you're going to live now.

—JOAN BAEZ

I have always had a dread of becoming a passenger in life.

—MARGARET II, QUEEN OF DENMARK

☺
130

In great moments, life seems neither right nor wrong, but something greater; it seems inevitable.

—MARGARET SHERWOOD

You are all you will ever have for certain.

—JUNE HAVOC

Finding your passion is about
connecting the dots between your
head and your heart.

—MARIA MARSALA

People are like stained glass windows.
They sparkle and shine when the sun is
out, but when the darkness sets in, their
true beauty is revealed only if there is light
from within.

—ELIZABETH KÜBLER-ROSS

☺
—
131

I have learned not to worry about love,
but to honor its coming with all my heart.

—ALICE WALKER

No trumpets sound when the important
decisions of our lives are made. Destiny is
made known silently.

—AGNES DE MILLE

Some women go through life turning
on lamps in the evening. Others are
themselves a light.

—HELEN PERKES

THE INGREDIENTS OF A
WONDERFUL LIFE

The kind of beauty I want most is the
hard-to-get kind that comes from within:
strength, courage, dignity.

—RUBY DEE

Life is a mystery as deep as ever
death can be.

—MARY MAPES DODGE

Eating is not merely a material pleasure.
Eating well gives a spectacular joy to life
and contributes immensely to good will
and happy companionship. It is of great
importance to the morale.

—ELSA SCHIAPARELLI

Good communication is just as
stimulating as black coffee, and just as
hard to sleep after.

—ANNE MORROW LINDBERGH

☺
—
133

The point is not to pay back kindness
but to pass it on.

—JULIA ALVAREZ

The things we truly love stay with
us always, locked in our hearts as long as
life remains.

—JOSEPHINE BAKER

The only thing that makes life possible is permanent, intolerable uncertainty; not knowing what comes next.

—URSULA K. LE GUIN

I'm not happy, I'm cheerful. There's a difference. A happy woman has no cares at all. a cheerful woman has cares but has learned how to deal with them.

—BEVERLY SILLS

☺
—
134

The universe is made of stories, not of atoms.

—MURIEL RUKEYSER

No one has a right to consume happiness without producing it.

—HELEN KELLER

Desire, ask, believe, receive.

—STELLA TERRILL MANN

Live as if you like yourself,
and it may happen.

—MARGE PIERCY

Choice is all we have.
Choice is all we need.

—KAREN CASEY

☺
—
135

Learn to trust your own judgment, learn
inner independence, learn to trust that
time will sort good from bad—including
your own bad.

—DORIS LESSING

The cure for boredom is curiosity.
There is no cure for curiosity.

—ELLEN PARR

Without an open-minded mind, you can
never be a great success.

—MARTHA STEWART

Grace, growth, and gratitude: these are my
highest aspirations.

—GLORIA ARLISS

"Yes" is contagious on a subliminal level. It
affects everything you do.

—SARK

Happily, love is a pleasant emotion and
thrives as well in stables as in palaces.

—DIANE ACKERMAN

Life is better than death, I believe, if only
because it is less boring, and because it
has fresh peaches in it.

—ALICE WALKER

COUNT ON YOUR OWN CHARACTER

Don't compromise yourself.
You are all you've got.

—JANIS JOPLIN

Civilization is a method of living and an
attitude of equal respect for all people.

—JANE ADDAMS

As long as you keep a person down,
some part of you has to be down there
to hold him down, so it means you cannot
soar as you otherwise might.

—MARIAN ANDERSON

I would rather die a meaningful death than
live a meaningless life.

—CORAZON AQUINO

Character builds slowly, but it can be torn
down with incredible swiftness.

—FAITH BALDWIN

You can stand tall without standing
on someone. You can be a victor without
having victims.

—HARRIET WOODS

We cannot afford not to fight for growth
and understanding, even when it is painful,
as it is bound to be.

—MAY SARTON

If you can't change your fate, change
your attitude.

—AMY TAN

Self-respect cannot be hunted….
It comes to us when we are alone,
in quiet moments, in quiet places, when
we suddenly realize that, knowing the
good, we have done it; knowing the
beautiful, we have served it; knowing the
truth, we have spoken it.

—WHITNEY GRISWOLD

The willingness to accept responsibility for
one's own life is the source from which
self-respect springs.

—JOAN DIDION

☺
—
139

My recipe for life is not being afraid
of myself, afraid of what I think,
or of my opinions.

—EARTHA KITT

LIVE IN YOUR PRIME ALL THE TIME

The hardest years are those between ten and seventy.

—HELEN HAYES

The history of all times, and of today especially, teaches that…women will be forgotten if they forget to think about themselves.

—LOUISE OTTO

Strive for Five—try to learn five new words a week; it keeps your brain active and helps your memory skills. Also, a wild woman with a very large vocabulary is a very potent combination.

—AUTUMN STEPHENS

So much has been said and sung of
beautiful young girls, why doesn't
somebody wake up to the
beauty of old women?

—HARRIET BEECHER STOWE

One's prime is elusive. You little girls,
when you grow up, must be on the alert
to recognize your prime at whatever time
of your life it may occur.

—MURIEL SPARK

141

The wisdom acquired with the passage of
time is a useless gift unless you share it.

—ESTHER WILLIAMS

I hope when this life is over, people will say of me, "She lived, she laughed, she loved with all that she was." Consider what you want people to remember of you and live accordingly.

—BARB ROGERS

I learned a woman is never an old woman.

—JONI MITCHELL

☺

If we had no winter, the spring would not be so pleasant; if we did not sometimes taste of adversity, prosperity would not be so welcome.

—ANNE BRADSTREET

Age is something that doesn't matter, unless you are a cheese.

—BILLIE BURKE

What a wonderful life I've had!
I only wish I'd realized it sooner.

—COLETTE

I am beautiful as I am. I am the shape that
was gifted. My breasts are no longer perky
and upright like when I was a teenager.
My hips are wider than those of a fashion
model. For this I am glad, for these are the
signs of a life lived.

— CINDY OLSEN

☺

What is amazing for a woman of my age is
that I change as the world is changing—and
changing very, very fast. I don't think my
mother had that opportunity to change.

—JEANNE MOREAU

The secret of staying young is to live
honestly, eat slowly, and lie about your age.

—LUCILLE BALL

GROW TO LEARN,
LEARN TO GROW

I don't want to get to the end of my life
and find that I lived just the length of it. I
want to have lived the width of it as well.

—DIANE ACKERMAN

A really strong woman accepts the war she
went through and is ennobled by her scars.

—CARLY SIMON

☺

Fortunately, psychoanalysis is not the only
way to resolve inner conflicts. Life itself
remains a very effective therapist.

—KAREN HORNEY

You must learn day by day, year by year,
to broaden your horizon. The more things
you love, the more you are interested in,
the more you enjoy, the more you are
indignant about, the more you have left
when anything happens.

—ETHEL BARRYMORE

People don't live nowadays;
they get about ten percent out of life.

—ISADORA DUNCAN

☺
—
145

Happiness must be cultivated.
It is like character. It is not a thing to be
safely let alone for a moment, or it will
run to weeds.

—ELIZABETH STUART PHELPS

One is not born a woman,
one becomes one.

—SIMONE DE BEAUVOIR

You need only claim the events of your
life to make yourself yours. When you
truly possess all that you have been and
done, which may take some time, you are
fierce with reality.

—FLORIDA SCOTT MAXWELL

Adventure is worthwhile in itself.

—AMELIA EARHART

☺

146

If we don't change, we don't grow.
If we don't grow, we are not really
living. Growth demands a temporary
surrender of security.

—GAIL SHEEHY

At the moment you are most in awe
of all there is about life that you
don't understand, you are closer to
understanding it all than at any other time.

—JANE WAGNER

Learn to get in touch with the silence
within yourself and know that everything
has a purpose. There are no mistakes, no
coincidences, all events are blessings given
to us to learn from.

☺

—ELIZABETH KÜBLER-ROSS

Mistakes are part of the dues
one pays for a full life.

—SOPHIA LOREN

Random acts of kindness—simple acts of generosity—are not only nice for other people, but they actually are healthy for you physically as well as spiritually. They reduce levels of stress hormones. So go ahead and make yourself and others happy today!

—MARY RUSKIN

Life engenders life.
Energy creates energy. It is by spending oneself that one becomes rich.

—SARAH BERNHARDT

Take Time to Check in With Yourself – Unplug (and Recharge!)

Forego using technological devices today. Texting your friend, watching your favorite show, checking your email—all can wait until tomorrow! Turn off your devices and turn on your senses! Read a book, cook a meal, and enjoy the outdoors by taking a walk or tending to your garden. Technology distracts us from the real world; it occupies our attention with game applications, chat rooms, social media websites, commercials, and so on. Want to know what's going on in the news? Read a newspaper. Be aware of the here and now by finding activities that don't require electricity or a battery. Make your own entertainment!

☺
149

Chapter Seven

Daring Greatly: Making Sure Your Creativity and Ideas Count

This is your life, only you can truly control your choices, and choosing to dare is the best way to achieve being good to yourself as well as to the world. Here are some suggestions for how you can ensure simple daring in your life:

★ Be the best you can be by your own standards

★ Surround yourself with people who inspire you and make you feel good

★ Focus on what you have, not what you lack

★ Remember that optimism trumps pessimism every time!

★ Smile often and genuinely

★ Be honest, both to yourself and to others

★ Help others

★ Embrace your past, live in the present, and look forward to what is yet to come

★ Make radical self-belief your motto. BELIEVE!

Think about what makes life worth living—risk, daring, courage, and growth.

Some people seem to have a knack for it. We say they march to their own drummer; we're wowed by their resilience in the face of criticism and adversity. If you are one of those people, it's time to share your secrets with the rest of us and be a cheerleader for the timid among us. And if you're not one of those people yet, remember that we can all choose to put ourselves on the line as we go after our dreams, and we can always try to use our mistakes as lessons on the road to success. Decide that what you want is more important than your fear of getting it, and there is no stopping you. Nothing ventured, nothing gained. Life's an adventure, so venture forth and reach for your dreams!

INNER STRENGTH

A sheltered life can be a daring life as well.
For all serious daring starts from within.

—EUDORA WELTY

I never realized until lately that women
were supposed to be the inferior sex.

—KATHARINE HEPBURN

It's better to be a lion for a day than a
sheep all your life.

—SISTER ELIZABETH KENNY

Our strength is often composed
of the weakness we're damned if we're
going to show.

—MIGNON MCLAUGHLIN

Men are taught to apologize for their
weaknesses, women for their strengths.

—LOIS WYSE

We women talk too much, nevertheless,
we only say half of what we know.

—NANCY ASTOR

There is a growing strength in women, but
it is in the forehead, not in the forearm.

—BEVERLY SILLS

I've been through it all, baby.
I'm mother courage.

—ELIZABETH TAYLOR

More than anything, I think as our country
matures, we recognize that women deserve
to be treated with respect and dignity.

—BARBARA BOXER

A woman is like a tea bag—
you can't tell how strong she is until you
put her in hot water.

—ELEANOR ROOSEVELT

Always be a first-rate version of yourself,
instead of a second-rate version
of somebody else.

—JUDY GARLAND

☺

Remember, no one can make you feel
inferior without your consent.

—ELEANOR ROOSEVELT

It's sexy to be competent.

—LETTY COTTIN POGREBIN

If you do things well, do them better. Be
daring, be first, be different, be just.

—ANITA RODDICK

You were once wild here.
Don't let them tame you.

—ISADORA DUNCAN

I'm tough, ambitious, and
I know exactly what I want.

—MADONNA

I think that women making no apology for
being women is very refreshing.

—DREW BARRYMORE

Real power is when you are doing exactly
what you are supposed to be doing the
best it can be done.

—OPRAH WINFREY

☺
156

SHAKING THINGS UP

If you think you are too
small to be effective, you have never
been in bed with a mosquito.

—BETTY REESE

We lift our voices as one; let all know, we
are here, and we intend to stay!

—NANCY FREDERICK

☺
—
157

Cautious, careful people
always casting about to preserve their
reputation or social standards never can
bring about reform. Those who are really
in earnest are willing to be anything or
nothing in the world's estimation…and
bear the consequences.

—SUSAN B. ANTHONY

We've chosen the path to equality,
don't let them turn us around.

—GERALDINE FERRARO

If particular care and attention are not
paid to the ladies, we are determined
to foment a rebellion, and will not hold
ourselves bound by any laws in which we
have no voice or representation.

—ABIGAIL ADAMS

Justice is better than chivalry
if we cannot have both.

—ALICE STONE BLACKWELL

I am in the world to change the world.

—MURIEL RUKEYSER

I believe in a lively disrespect for most
forms of authority.

—RITA MAE BROWN

I prefer liberty to chains of diamonds.

—LADY MARY WORTLEY MONTAGU

Women belong in the house…
and the Senate.

—ANN RICHARDS

What is enough? Enough is when
somebody says, 'Get me the best people
you can find' and nobody notices when
half of them turn out to be women.

—LOUISE RENNE

You can't get swept off your feet if you are sitting down. Stand up and be noticed!

—CLAIRE CAMDEN

Men have always been afraid that women could get along without them.

—MARGARET MEAD

It's been a lot of fun
making the revolution.

—BETTY FRIEDAN

I'll not listen to reason. Reason always means what someone else has got to say.

—ELIZABETH GASKILL

BE A BAD GIRL IN
A GOOD WAY

Good girls go to heaven, bad girls
go everywhere.

—HELEN GURLEY BROWN

Well-behaved women
rarely make history.

—LAUREL THATCHER ULRICH

☺
161

I do not want people to be agreeable, as it
saves me the trouble of liking them.

—JANE AUSTEN

Only good girls keep diaries.
Bad girls don't have time.

—TALLULAH BANKHEAD

When the sun comes up,
I have morals again.

—ELAYNE BOOSLER

A woman can look both moral and
exciting…if she also looks as if it was
quite a struggle.

—EDNA FERBER

☺

162

Rules are for people who don't know how
to get around them.

—TORI HARRISON

I have too many fantasies to be a
housewife. I guess I am a fantasy.

—MARILYN MONROE

One wonders what would happen
in a society in which there were no rules
to break. Doubtless everyone would
quickly die of boredom.

—SUSAN HOWITCH

I am not eccentric. It's just that I am more
alive than most people. I am an unpopular
electric eel set in a pond of goldfish.

—DAME EDITH SITWELL

☺

163

Women are the real
architects of society.

—HARRIET BEECHER STOWE

I'm extraordinarily patient provided I can
get my own way in the end.

—MARGARET THATCHER

I've always taken risks, and never worried
what the world might really think of me.

—CHER

I can, therefore I am.

—SIMONE WEIL

Some say the glass is half empty,
some say the glass is half full; I say, are you
going to drink that?"

—LISA CLAYMEN

☺
—
164

If I had to live my life again, I'd make the
same mistakes, only sooner.

—TALLULAH BANKHEAD

Until you lose your reputation, you never
realize what a burden it was or what
freedom really is.

—MARGARET MITCHELL

FACING CHALLENGES

I'm not afraid of storms,
for I'm learning to sail my ship.

—LOUISA MAY ALCOTT

You can't be brave if you've only had
wonderful things happen to you.

—MARY TYLER MOORE

Remember that fear is something learned.
None of us are born afraid.

—MARY STANYAN

Whatever women do they must do twice
as well as men to be thought half as good.
Luckily, this is not difficult.

—CHARLOTTE WHITTON

If you want anything said, ask a man. If you want something done, ask a woman.

—MARGARET THATCHER

The naked truth is always better than the best-dressed lie.

—ANN LANDERS

If it's a woman, it's caustic; if it's a man, it's authoritative.

—BARBARA WALTERS

☺

If Rosa Parks had taken a poll before she sat down on that bus in Montgomery, she'd still be standing.

—MARY FRANCES BERRY

I once complained to my father that I didn't seem to be able to do things the same way other people did. Dad's advice? 'Margo, don't be a sheep. People hate sheep. They eat sheep.'

—MARGO KAUFMAN

Speak up for yourself, or you'll end up a rug.

—MAE WEST

And the trouble is, if you don't risk anything, you risk more.

—ERICA JONG

UNLEASH YOUR DESIRE AND REACH FOR YOUR STARS

It is our choices…that show what we
truly are, far more than our abilities.

—J.K. ROWLING

When you have a dream, you've got to
grab it and never let it go.

—CAROL BURNETT

I think the key is for women not
to set any limits.

—MARTINA NAVRATILOVA

There are no dangerous thoughts; thinking
itself is dangerous.

—HANNAH ARENDT

Truth is always exciting. Speak it, then;
life is dull without it.

—PEARL S. BUCK

Be bold. If you're going to make
an error, make a doozy, and don't be
afraid to hit the ball.

—BILLIE JEAN KING

Be bold in what you stand for
and careful what you fall for.

—RUTH BOORSTIN

To tell a woman everything she may not
do is to tell her what she can do.

—UNKNOWN

You may be imperious, but the effect is
always spoiled when you apologize.

—KAREN WILLIAMS

Real women don't have flushes, they have power surges.

—SANDRA CABOT

When you believe in your dreams you are able to fight for them.

—CECILY BARRY

All good fortune is a gift of the gods, and you don't win the favor of the ancient gods by being good, but by being bold.

—ANITA BROOKNER

The thing women have yet to learn is nobody gives you power. You just take it.

—ROSEANNE BARR

If you don't act as if your name were on the door, it never will be.

—PATRICIA FRIPP

It's hard to be free, but when it works,
it is sure worth it.

—JANIS JOPLIN

Bite off more than you can chew,
then chew it.

—ELLA WILLIAMS

The most effective way to do it,
is to do it.

—AMELIA EARHART

☺

Life shrinks or expands in proportion
to one's courage.

—ANAÏS NIN

Catch People Doing Something Right
(and Make Sure They Know It!)

During stressful times or difficult transitions, our
natural tendency is often to contract and grow rigid.
In this mindset, we seem to only be able to focus
on the negatives. We think about the despair and
torment of the death of a loved one, but not the
wonderful moments spent together. We think of
the heartbreak of a relationship ending, but not of
the exhilaration and freedom of being unattached.
We might even scold our loved ones, our friends, or
our coworkers for something minor or insignificant
when we wallow in such negativity. But it is in these
moments specifically that gratitude can be used to
alter this way of thinking.

Finding positives and accentuating
them is the easiest way to turn those proverbial
frowns upside down and gray skies back to blue.
Try catching someone doing something right for a
change, not something wrong. Giving praise for a job
well done lifts all parties involved and is the easiest
and perhaps best way to say, "Thank you" without
actually having to say it.

Chapter Eight

Women Make All the Difference at Work

Instead of writing up and crossing things off of your to-do list or a "bucket list," create a "life list." Let your hopes, dreams, fears, and thoughts spill out of you and onto this list. Next to each entry, write down how that emotion or fear makes you feel—does it hold you back or empower you? This task will put you on the road to self-discovery. Knowing who you are is important in order to have relationships with others. Know thyself. And use this knowledge to up your effectiveness.

I've gotten into reading biographies and autobiographies of people whose lives and work inspire me. I've noticed that even in the case of the "overnight successes," you have to get at least halfway through the book of someone's life story before their hard work starts to pay off in any substantial way. I'm talking chapter after chapter of working for no recognition, no pay, and no glory; years or even decades of disappointments, detours, and being down in the dumps. But these people struggle through; some even find joy in the adversity. And somewhere in my reading, I think, "Right, of course!"

Pay, glory, and recognition are all great, but they aren't real motivators. If that's all you're working toward, you're probably never going to get there. Doing what you love and loving what you do is the real point. Then all that other stuff can be icing on the cake if and when it comes around. And even if you never get the kudos you deserve, you'll hardly notice as you chug along reaping the rewards of a challenging, interesting career.

Dream up a goal, make a plan, and stay present in the moment as you work it out. Evaluate yourself and those around you honestly as you go, and keep the bigger picture in the forefront of your mind. You're going to have to think up new ways to work around obstacles, and you're going to have to battle some drudgery. That might be the hardest part. One way is to keep a reminder of your goals close at hand—a picture, a poem, a sketch— and look at it to help motivate you through the boring stuff. Get your nose onto the grindstone, and watch as your worries fall away. Get your hands a little dirty and you'll be well on your way to being the best you can be.

WORK AS IF IT'S FULFILLING

Work itself is the reward. If I choose
challenging work, it will pay me back with
interest....This attempt for excellence
is what sustains the most well-lived and
satisfying, successful lives.

—MERYL STREEP

People think at the end of the day that a
man is the only answer [to fulfillment.]
Actually, a job is better for me.

—DIANA, PRINCESS OF WALES

Nothing gratifies one more than to be
admired for doing what one likes.

—DOROTHY L. SAYERS

I've never been a fan of work as it's usually defined by other people. But when I learned how to define it for myself, I realized that it actually can be as fulfilling as I'd always hoped.

—BELINDA CASSIDY

Look at a day when you are supremely satisfied at the end of it. it's not a day when you lounge around doing nothing; it's when you've had everything to do, and you've done it.

—MARGARET THATCHER

Work won't always make your heart sing. But when it does, it's one of the best feelings there is.

—AMY PORTER

☺
—
178

To follow without halt, one aim;
there is the secret of success. And
success? What is it? I do not find it in the
applause of the theater; it lies rather in
the satisfaction of accomplishment.

—ANNA PAVLOVA

Laziness may appear attractive,
but work gives satisfaction.

—ANNE FRANK

☺

179

I look back on my life like a good day's
work; it was done and I am satisfied with it.

—GRANDMA MOSES

What we really want to do is what we
are really meant to do. When we do what
we are meant to do, money comes to us,
doors open for us, we feel useful, and the
work we do feels like play to us.

—JULIA CAMERON

You are not in business to be popular.

—KIRSTIE ALLEY

The most popular labor-saving
device is still money.

—PHYLLIS GEORGE

Work is the world's easiest
escape from boredom and the only
surefire road to success.

—MARABEL MORGAN

The ability to control one's own destiny…
comes from constant hard
work and courage.

—MAYA ANGELOU

To fulfill a dream, to be allowed to sweat
over lonely labor, to be given a chance to
create, is the meat and potatoes of life.
The money is the gravy.

—BETTE DAVIS

Measure not the work until the day's
out and the labor is done.

—ELIZABETH BARRETT BROWNING

Women hold up half the sky.

—CHINESE PROVERB

Instead of thinking about where you are,
think about where you want to be. It takes
twenty years of hard work to become an
overnight success.

—DIANA RANKIN

What I know is, is that if you do work
that you love, and the work fulfills you, the
rest will come.

—OPRAH WINFREY

FIND YOUR BALANCE

You cannot be really first-rate at your
work if your work is all you are.

—ANNA QUINDLEN

☺
—
182

I believe you are your work. Don't trade
the stuff of your life, time, for nothing
more than dollars. That's a rotten bargain.

—RITA MAE BROWN

Take your work seriously,
but never yourself.

—MARGOT FONTEYN

Any woman who has a career and a family
automatically develops something in the
way of two personalities, like two sides of
a dollar bill, each different in design…. Her
problem is to keep one from draining the
life from the other.

—IVY BAKER PRIEST

A human being must have occupation
if he or she is not to become a nuisance
to the world.

—DOROTHY L. SAYERS

Value work. But not any kind of work.
Ask yourself, "Is the work vital,
strengthening my own character, or
inspiring others, or helping the world?"

—ANNA ROBERTSON BROWN

WORK SMART AND STICK IT OUT

Women have to be a lot smarter and brighter and have to work a lot harder to prepare themselves. They have to watch what they do and how they behave. It's not a free world yet.

—LETITIA BALDRIDGE

The test for whether or not you can hold a job should not be the arrangement of your chromosomes.

—CONGRESSWOMAN BELLA ABZUG

Nighttime is really the best time to work. All the ideas are there to be yours because everyone else is asleep.

—CATHERINE O'HARA

Hard work need not always be a chore.
At least not outside the house.

—JENNIFER CROWLEY

All work done mindfully rounds us out,
helps complete us as persons.

—MARSHA SINETAR

When her last child is off to school, we
don't want the talented woman wasting
her time in work far below her capacity.
We want her to come out running.

—MARY INGRAHAM BUNTING

I am independent! I can live alone,
and I love to work.

—MARY CASSATT

I hate housework. You make the beds, you wash the dishes, and six months later you have to start all over again.

—JOAN RIVERS

People have to feel needed. Frequently, we just offer a job and "perks." We don't always offer people a purpose. When people feel there is a purpose and that they're needed, there's not much else to do except let them do the work.

—MAYA ANGELOU

The days you work are the best days.

—GEORGIA O'KEEFFE

To work in the world lovingly means that we are defining what we will be for, rather than reacting to what we are against.

—CHRISTINA BALDWIN

Personally, I have nothing against work,
particularly when performed quietly and
unobtrusively by someone else. I just don't
happen to think it's an appropriate subject
for an 'ethic.'

—BARBARA EHRENREICH

If hard work were such a wonderful
thing, surely the rich would have kept it all
to themselves.

—LANE KIRKLAND

☺

187

Always be smarter than the people
who hire you.

—LENA HORNE

Work is something you can count on,
a trusted lifelong friend who never
deserts you.

—MARGARET BOURKE-WHITE

Rather than sit around, I'll work.

—KELLY LYNCH

I work as often as I want and
yet I'm free as a bird.

—ETHEL MERMAN

…look and listen hard, do not be
discouraged by rejections—we've all had
them many times—and revise your work.

—JOYCE CAROL OATES

Attempt the impossible in order
to improve your work.

—BETTE DAVIS

Aerodynamically the bumblebee shouldn't
be able to fly, but the bumblebee doesn't
know that, so it goes on flying anyway.

—MARY KAY ASH

☺
—
188

Yesterday I dared to struggle.
Today I dare to win.

—BERNADETTE DEVLIN

Plan your work for today and every day,
then work your plan.

—MARGARET THATCHER

There are two kinds of people, those who
do the work and those who take credit.
Try to be in the first group, there is less
competition there.

—INDIRA GANDHI

☺
—
189

Opportunities are often
disguised as hard work, so most people
don't recognize them.

—ANN LANDERS

I would rather make mistakes in kindness
and compassion than work miracles in
unkindness and hardness.

—MOTHER TERESA

Goals are dreams within deadlines.

—DIANA SCHARF HUNT

APPLY SOME ELBOW GREASE

The biggest sin is sitting on your ass.

—FLORYNCE KENNEDY

When it comes to getting things done, we
need fewer architects and more bricklayers.

—COLLEEN C. BARRETT

By and large, mothers and housewives
are the only workers who do not have
regular time off. They are the great
vacationless class.

—ANNE MORROW LINDBERGH

Don't feel entitled to anything you
didn't sweat and struggle for.

—MARIAN WRIGHT EDELMAN

☺

191

Nobody ever drowned
in his own sweat.

—ANN LANDERS

Luck? I don't know anything about luck.
I've never banked on it, and I'm afraid of
people who do. Luck to me is something
else: hard work—and realizing what is
opportunity and what isn't.

—LUCILLE BALL

The only thing that ever sat its way
to success was a hen.

—SARAH BROWN

The sweat of hard work is not to be
displayed. It is much more graceful to
appear favored by the gods.

—MAXINE HONG KINGSTON

☺

192

Whatever muscles I have are the product
of my own hard work and nothing else.

—EVELYN ASHFORD

Inspiration usually comes during work,
rather than before it.

—MADELEINE L'ENGLE

Creativity comes from trust.
Trust your instincts. And never hope
more than you work."

—RITA MAE BROWN

I didn't have to work until I was three.
But after that, I never stopped.

—MARTHA RAYE

About the only thing that comes
to us without effort is old age.

—GLORIA PITZER

☺

193

Nothing will work unless you do.

—MAYA ANGELOU

FOR THE LOVE OF IT

Work is either fun or drudgery. It depends
on your attitude. I like fun.

—COLLEEN C. BARRETT

Career is too pompous a word. It was a
job, and I have always felt privileged to be
paid for what I love doing.

—BARBARA STANWYCK

You know you are on the road
to success if you would do your job
and not be paid for it.

—OPRAH WINFREY

All the things I love is
what my business is about.

—MARTHA STEWART

To love what you do and feel that it
matters—how could anything
be more fun?

—KATHERINE GRAHAM

Your Goals Will Grow You

Make a list of short-term goals you would like to
achieve by the end of the year, month, or even week.
As you accomplish your goals, give gratitude for the
effort, inspiration, people, and other factors that
helped you along the way. My goal is to see how I can
give more to those around me, near and far. I would
love to hear your aspirations!

☺

195

Chapter Nine

Never Hold Back: Shine Your Light Each and Every Day!

We all need reminders now and then. You don't leap out of bed every day knowing you are amazing and about to have an incredible day. All of us have a lot of demands, pressures, to-do tasks, and responsibilities, so we find ourselves rushing around, working hard to please others. Most of the time, you find yourself at the back of your own bus, having made everyone else happy but your own damn self. Then you go and beat yourself up about it.

Let's stop that, shall we?

I'm here to remind you that you are pretty darn great. I had to learn to remind myself of that, but you know what? It feels pretty darn good. It is even kind of addictive in the best possible way. While this might seem like a fluffy little exercise, it actually runs quite deep and will serve you the rest of your life. There are reasons we need esteem boosters here and there; we pick up scars along the way and get bumps and bruises in the wake of the stress of daily life. If you had a bad childhood, you have these old "tapes" from poor parenting that loop around in your brain on an unconscious level: "You'll never amount to anything. You're not good at sports. Your sister has a much better singing voice than you, so we're sending her to music camp, and you can stay behind and babysit." Even really nice moms and dads perpetrate these parenting errors that leave marks on the souls of their children. So you need to make it one of your daily habits to keep affirming yourself. No matter what, keep forging ahead, knowing you are fabulous!

~~~

Keep making great strides in the face of adversity. Holding down the fort while dreaming up the next great thing. Hurtling over massive barriers to your success with creative leaps and bounds. Just think: women have been doing this since the beginning of time, and it doesn't look to be slowing down any time soon. You may cram more into your day and get paid less for it, get fewer big breaks, and struggle to make your ideas heard, but you know what? You're up to this challenge.

But wait. In creeps fear, in slithers self-doubt. Are we more susceptible to these, too? Maybe so, because we're in tune with our feelings and those of the people around us. But we have to remember that the flip side of our self-doubt is our ability to empathize—the emotional intelligence that serves us in every relationship we have, from the bedroom to the boardroom. And let's be honest with ourselves. As Marianne Williamson put it so well, "Our deepest fear is not that we are inadequate. Our deepest fear is that we are powerful beyond measure." Know yourself, and don't hold back. Give yourself permission to find the best of you and let it shine without shame or apology. Nobody's going to benefit from your hesitation—you've got too much to get done to keep your talents hidden away so that others are more comfortable around you.

Dare to be powerful. Try it out. All those *clichés*—roll with the punches, just do it, you'll never know until you try, you can do anything you set your mind to—well, they get stuck in our heads because they're true. So go for it!

☺
—
199

BELIEVE IN YOURSELF

To believe in something not yet proved and to underwrite it with our lives: it is the only way we can leave the future open.

—LILLIAN SMITH

Only with a steady heart can true excellence be reached.

—MOIRA LANDON

I can honestly say that I was never affected by the question of the success of an undertaking. If I felt it was the right thing to do, I was for it regardless of the possible outcome.

—GOLDA MEIR

Everyone has talent. What is rare is the courage to follow talent to the dark place where it leads.

—ERICA JONG

It's not so much how busy you are, but why you are busy. The bee is praised; the mosquito is swatted.

—MARIE O'CONNER

☺
201

Do not follow where the path may lead. Go instead where there is no path and leave a trail.

—MURIEL STRODE

One must fight for a life of action, not reaction.

—RITA MAE BROWN

A sobering thought: what if, at this very
moment, I am living up to my full potential?

—JANE WAGNER

Women share with men the need for
personal success, even the taste of power,
and no longer are we willing to satisfy
those needs through the achievements of
surrogates, whether husbands, children, or
merely role models.

—ELIZABETH DOLE

☺

202

Please know that I am quite aware of the
hazards. Women must try to do things
as men have tried. When they fail, their
failure must be but a challenge to others.

—AMELIA EARHART

The most alluring thing a woman can have
is confidence.

—BEYONCÉ KNOWLES-CARTER

Inaction, contrary to its reputation as being
a refuge, is neither safe nor comfortable.

—MADELINE KUHN

Getting ahead in a difficult profession
requires avid faith in yourself. That is why
some people with mediocre talent, but
with great inner drive, go much further
than people with vastly superior talent.

—SOPHIA LOREN

203

It is above all by the imagination
that we achieve perception and
compassion and hope.

—URSULA K. LE GUIN

I have dreamed in my life, dreams that have stayed with me after, and changed my ideas; they have gone through and through me, like wine through water, and altered the color of my mind.

—EMILY BRONTË

Believe in yourself: across all ages, studies have shown that a solid belief in one's own abilities increases life satisfaction by over 40 [percent] and makes us happier both in our work and home lives.

—MEG DESMOND

OVERCOMING CHALLENGES AND FEARS

You gain strength, courage,
and confidence by every experience in
which you really stop to look fear in the
face....You must do the thing you think
you cannot do.

—ELEANOR ROOSEVELT

You may be disappointed if you fail, but
you are doomed if you don't try.

—BEVERLY SILLS

You can do one of two things: just shut
up, which is something I don't find easy, or
learn an awful lot very fast, which is what
I tried to do.

—JANE FONDA

☺
—

If we are to achieve a richer culture,
rich in contrasting values, we must
recognize the whole gamut of human
potentialities, and so weave a less arbitrary
social fabric, one in which each diverse
gift will find a fitting place.

—MARGARET MEAD

It irritates me to be told how things
have always been done. I defy the tyranny
of precedent. I cannot afford the luxury of
a closed mind. I go for anything that might
improve the past.

—CLARA BARTON

You can't build a reputation on
what you intend to do.

—LIZ SMITH

Success will come to you in direct
proportion to the number of times you
are willing to risk failure.

—PAT GURITZ

Because I am a woman, I must
make unusual efforts to succeed. If I fail,
no one will say, "She doesn't have what it
takes." They will say, "Women don't have
what it takes."

—CLARE BOOTHE LUCE

I really don't think life is about the I-could-
have-beens. Life is only about the I-tried-
to-dos. I don't mind the failure, but I can't
imagine that I'd forgive myself if
I didn't try.

—NIKKI GIOVANNI

A champion is afraid of losing.
Everyone else is afraid of winning.

—BILLIE JEAN KING

You'll never do a whole lot unless
you're brave enough to try.

—DOLLY PARTON

Risk! Risk anything! Care no more for the
opinion of others, for those voices.
Do the hardest thing on earth for you.
Act for yourself. Face the truth.

—KATHERINE MANSFIELD

When I dare to be powerful—to use my
strength in the service of my vision—
then it becomes less and less important
whether or not I am afraid.

—AUDRE LORDE

If you just set out to be liked, you would
be prepared to compromise on anything at
any time, and you would achieve nothing.

—MARGARET THATCHER

SWEET SUCCESSES

Fearless women go to the top.

—BEYONCÉ KNOWLES-CARTER

☺

209

For what is done or learned by
one class of women becomes, by virtue
of their common womanhood, the
property of all women.

—ELIZABETH BLACKWELL

Not only have women been successful in
entering fields in which men are supposed
to have a more natural aptitude, but they
have created entirely new businesses.

—LUCRETIA P. HUNTER

Winning may not be everything, but losing
has little to recommend it.

—SENATOR DIANNE FEINSTEIN

☺

210

The worst part of success is to try to find
someone who is happy for you.

—BETTE MIDLER

The women of today are the thoughts
of their mothers and grandmothers,
embodied and made alive. They are active,
capable, determined, and bound to win…
millions of women dead and gone are
speaking through us today.

—MATILDA JOSLYN GAGE

Security is not the meaning of my life.
Great opportunities are worth the risk.

—SHIRLEY HUFSTEDLER

I don't think any change in the world has
been more significant than the change in
the status of women....A woman's world
was her home, her family, and perhaps a
little community service. Today, a woman's
world is as broad as the universe.

—BELLE S. SPAFFORD

☺
—
211

If I had learned to type, I never would have
made brigadier general.

—ELIZABETH P. HOISINGTOM

Don't confuse "things" with success—you are neither better nor worse for where you live, what you drive, or the size of your bank account. Remember what really matters in your life—and it is not 'stuff.'

—MARY JANE RYAN

Getting to the top isn't bad, and it's probably best done as an afterthought.

—ANNE WILSON SCHAEF

☺

TAKE LITTLE STEPS, MAKE HUGE STRIDES

Success is not a doorway, it's a staircase.

—DOTTIE WALTERS

I am only one; but still I am one.
I cannot do everything, but still I can do
something. I will not refuse to do the
something I can do.

—HELEN KELLER

We must not, in trying to think about how
we can make a big difference, ignore the
small daily differences we can make, which
over time add up to big differences that
we often cannot foresee.

—MARIAN WRIGHT EDELMAN

Don't wait for your ship to come in and
feel angry and cheated when it doesn't.
Get going with something small.

—IRENE KASSORLA

☺

How wonderful it is that nobody needs to
wait a single moment before starting to
improve the world.

—ANNE FRANK

Do not wait for leaders; do it alone,
person to person.

—MOTHER TERESA

☺

I'm always moving forward.

—DEBBIE ALLEN

I believe the choice to be excellent
begins with aligning your thoughts and
words with the intention to require more
from yourself.

—OPRAH WINFREY

Strive for excellence, each and every day.

—MARION CONDIT

NEVER GIVE UP

Just don't give up trying to do what you really want to do. Where there is love and inspiration, I don't think you can go wrong.

—ELLA FITZGERALD

Always continue the climb. It is possible for you to do whatever you choose, if you first get to know who you are and are willing to work with a power that is greater than ourselves to achieve it.

—ELLA WHEELER WILCOX

Something which we think is impossible now is not impossible in another decade.

—CONSTANCE BAKER MOTLEY

When I stand before God at the end of
my life, I would hope that I would not have
a single bit of talent left and could say,
"I used everything you gave me."

—ERMA BOMBECK

I never see what has been done; I only see
what remains to be done.

—MARIE CURIE

☺

The way I see it, if you want the rainbow,
you gotta put up with the rain.

—DOLLY PARTON

Human successes, like human failures, are
composed of one action at a time and
achieved by one person at a time.

—PATSY H. SAMPSON

I think one's feelings waste themselves in words; they ought all to be distilled into actions which bring results.

—FLORENCE NIGHTINGALE

The only sin is mediocrity.

—MARTHA GRAHAM

Perseverance is failing nineteen times and succeeding the twentieth.

—JULIE ANDREWS

☺
217

Learning is not attained by chance, it must be sought for with ardor and diligence.

—ABIGAIL ADAMS

I'm not going to limit myself because people won't accept the fact that I can do something else.

—DOLLY PARTON

No matter how tough, no matter what kind of outside pressure, no matter how many bad breaks along the way, I must keep my sights on the final goal, to win… with more love and passion than the world has ever witnessed in any performance.

—BILLIE JEAN KING

If you don't like something, change it. If you can't change it, change your attitude. Don't complain.

—MAYA ANGELOU

There's a big difference between seeing an opportunity and seizing an opportunity.

—PAT GURITZ

We can do anything we want to do if we stick with it long enough.

—HELEN KELLER

Do You Know How Great You Are?

Compliment someone today, and mean it. A genuine compliment can boost someone's confidence and that is a great feeling. If you like your coworker's blouse or new haircut (or both!), tell her. Open and honest communication works wonders for developing relationships and makes everybody's day a little bit nicer. Take the time to let someone know that you appreciate having her or him in your life. Sometimes we forget how good it feels to be appreciated; yet we know how lousy it feels to be unappreciated. Go ahead and tell someone how thankful you are for her or his presence in your life; it will only make you closer. Wonderful things can happen when you affirm the people in your life.

Conclusion

Three Life-Changing Pieces of Advice I Am Passing On to You

In closing, I want to give you the three best pieces of advice I have ever received. One is to get up earlier each day, the second is to stop complaining, and the last is about being grateful, no matter what.

Get Up a Half Hour Earlier Each Day

This simple suggestion from Peter Shankman at a publishing conference ended up being a life-changing piece of advice. He said when he tried this, it transformed his life, and it is as simple as this: get up a half hour earlier, and use that time to reach out to people. He said it can be as easy as wishing a happy birthday to your Facebook contacts, one meaningful phone call first thing in the morning, or writing a personal note to someone you have longed to be in contact with. I remember listening to him and thinking that I really didn't want to get up any earlier, that my days were long enough, and that it did not sound that appealing. But his sincerity and enthusiasm somehow broke through my "baditude," and I pondered the idea as I walked back to my car and drove across the Bay Bridge back to my office. I decided to try it, and I can tell you, he is RIGHT.

That extra half hour every morning has been one of the best investments I ever made, so much so that I added an hour. It completely changed my life for the better. Try it!

Stop Complaining

Go one day without complaining; even better, go a week. If this is hard for you to accomplish, it's time to make some changes in your life. Think positively, live in the present, and appreciate where you are and who you are. Today is a gift, accept and embrace it. Will Bowen authored a fantastic book on this very topic, *A Complaint Free World,* which I turn to when I need a reminder, as all of us do now and again. My copy came with a bracelet, a simple way to monitor how often you complain that helps you track your progress toward becoming "complaint-free." Put on the bracelet, and every time you complain, switch it to the other wrist. The goal is to go twenty-one consecutive days without complaining or switching the side where you wear the bracelet. It is harder than you might think, and I was a bit shocked at what a complainer I turned out to be. It was a really good exercise for me, and I highly recommend it. I benefited enormously from it, and I suspect the people around me did, too!

Have an Attitude of Gratitude

1. Be grateful and recognize the things others have done to help you.

2. When you say, "Thank you" to someone, it signals what you appreciate and why you appreciate it.

3. Post a "Thank you to all" on your Facebook page or your blog, or send individual emails to friends, family, and colleagues.

4. Send a handwritten thank-you note. These are noteworthy because so few of us take time to write and mail them in our modern age.

5. Think thoughts of gratitude—two or three good things that happened today—and notice how calm settles through your head, at least for a moment. It activates a part of the brain that floods the body with endorphins, or feel-good hormones.

6. Remember the ways your life has been made easier or better because of others' efforts. Be aware of and acknowledge the good things, large and small, going on around you.

7. Keep a gratitude journal, or set aside time each day or evening to list the people or things you're grateful for today. The list may start out short, but it will grow as you notice more of the good things around you.

8. Being grateful shakes you out of self-absorption and helps you recognize those who've done wonderful things for you. Expressing that gratitude continues to draw those people into your sphere.

9. Remember this thought from Maya Angelou: "When you learn, teach; when you get, give."

10. Join forces to do good. If you have survived illness or loss, you may want to reach out to others to help as a way of showing gratitude for those who reached out to you.

☺
—
224

About the Author

Becca Anderson comes from a long line of preachers and teachers from Ohio and Kentucky. The teacher side of her family led Becca to become a women's studies scholar who writes *The Blog of Awesome Women*. An avid collector of meditations, prayers, and blessings, she helps run a "Gratitude and Grace Circle" that meets monthly at homes, churches, and bookstores. Becca Anderson credits her spiritual practice with helping in her recovery from cancer and wants to share this with anyone who is facing difficulty in their life. The author of *Think Happy to Stay Happy*, *Real Life Mindfulness*, and *Every Day Thankful*, Becca Anderson shares her inspirational writings and suggested acts of kindness at https://thedailyinspoblog. wordpress.com/.

☺